SpringerBriefs in Cybersecurity

T0183926

For further volumes:
http://www.springer.com/series/10634

Cybersecurity is a difficult and complex field. The technical, political and legal questions surrounding it are complicated, often stretching a spectrum of diverse technologies, varying legal bodies, different political ideas and responsibilities. Cybersecurity is intrinsically interdisciplinary, and most activities in one field immediately affect the others. Technologies and techniques, strategies and tactics, motives and ideologies, rules and laws, institutions and industries, power and money—all of these topics have a role to play in cybersecurity, and all of these are tightly interwoven.

The SpringerBriefs in Cybersecurity series is comprised of two types of briefs: topic- and country-specific briefs. Topic-specific briefs strive to provide a comprehensive coverage of the whole range of topics surrounding cybersecurity, combining whenever possible legal, ethical, social, political and technical issues. Authors with diverse backgrounds explain their motivation, their mindset, and their approach to the topic, to illuminate its theoretical foundations, the practical nuts and bolts and its past, present and future. Country-specific briefs cover national perceptions and strategies, with officials and national authorities explaining the background, the leading thoughts and interests behind the official statements, to foster a more informed international dialogue.

Heli Tiirmaa-Klaar · Jan Gassen
Elmar Gerhards-Padilla · Peter Martini

Botnets

Heli Tiirmaa-Klaar
Expert in Cybersecurity
Tallinn
Estonia

Jan Gassen
Research Group Cyber Defense
Fraunhofer FKIE
Bonn
Germany

Elmar Gerhards-Padilla
Research Group Cyber Defense
Fraunhofer FKIE
Bonn
Germany

Peter Martini
Director Fraunhofer FKIE
Fraunhofer FKIE
Bonn
Germany

ISSN 2193-973X   ISSN 2193-9748   (electronic)
ISBN 978-1-4471-5215-6   ISBN 978-1-4471-5216-3   (eBook)
DOI 10.1007/978-1-4471-5216-3
Springer London Heidelberg New York Dordrecht

Library of Congress Control Number: 2013938271

Printed on acid-free paper

Springer is part of Springer Science+Business Media (www.springer.com)

Foreword

SpringerBriefs in Cybersecurity aim to provide the cybersecurity debate with a scientific foundation. Every single brief is designed to give a comprehensive, intelligible, yet scientific and objective insight into the specific topic it covers. In addition to this particular outset, the Briefs also want to cover their topics from a number of different angles whenever suitable. Especially the combination of technical and non-technical expertise is considered to be of high importance.

Botnets adheres to these guidelines. It combines a technical survey on botnets, on their immediate technical structures, the methods used in botnet-related activities and technical means to detect and to remove botnets, with a political and strategic survey, giving an insight into the problem from a political and legal point of view. Both surveys have been written by separate authors, but guided by a dialogue between those authors, in order to map technical onto political problems and vice versa and to avoid redundancies. The result is a real brief. It is a briefing on botnets, which covers almost every possible aspect of this topic. It enables the reader to understand the problems associated with botnets, the technical and political approaches to solve or at least to mitigate the problem, and to identify suitable points to delve deeper into subject and learn more about relevant details.

Botnets are not among the top ranking technical threats in the cyber domain, and they are not as popular any more as they used to be. But they still provide a basis for many cybercrime business models and loom large in Internet resource depletion attacks such as the well-known "distributed denial of service" technique, which is frequently used by hacktivists for visible online protesting. It is of ongoing importance to understand and to judge botnets, their technicalities and the political and legal process, which constitutes the larger part of the fight against botnets. And there is an interesting systematic aspect to botnets. As one of the most established threats, this problem has received a lot of attention and activity over the years. Taking a look at this very process—which is illustrated in detail in this brief—provides an intriguing insight of how technological innovation and policy making in cybersecurity work and interact. This knowledge will clearly be beneficial for future debates on botnets as on other threats and cyber topics at large.

Sandro Gaycken

Contents

Botnets, Cybercrime and National Security

Heli Tiirmaa-Klaar

Abstract This chapter will address how botnet infrastructure could be exploited for national security and cybercrime purposes. Cyber threats, including botnets, represent a fast developing international issue that is facilitated by the low aware-ness of end-users, by differences in national legal and policy approaches to cyber security and by the lack of attention to security in companies providing Internet services. Botnets are used for reaping economic gains by criminals as well as for politically motivated activities. Although many efforts have been made recently in mitigating botnets, they will be likely to re-emerge at the new level of sophis-tication and organisation. Also, botnet activity will move away from developed countries and spread further in emerging markets and in developing countries. The following study approaches the subject as a public policy issue and will analyse the phenomenon of botnets from national security, law enforcement and regulatory policy perspective. It will also offer recommendations for policy-makers on differ-ent public policy responses to effectively fight botnets, and highlights the need for international response mechanisms. In order to successfully address cyber threats, law enforcement capacity building and criminal justice should be strengthened globally, with a special focus on fast growing emerging economies.

1 Introduction

Never before has technology outpaced the ability of mankind to find efficient poli-cies and governance mechanisms as witnessed in cyberspace related issues. ICT revolution and the development of the World Wide Web has accelerated economic growth, brought social justice and political opportunities. It has changed the way how we see the world today and do our daily business. Democratic movements spurring up in formerly repressive regimes were supported by ICT technology. Poor regions in the developing countries have been able to trade their goods. Small and medium sized businesses in industrial countries have found markets world-wide. For all of these positive developments, the ICT has been a great enabler.

H. Tiirmaa-Klaar et al., *Botnets*, SpringerBriefs in Cybersecurity,
DOI: 10.1007/978-1-4471-5216-3_1, © The Author(s) 2013

Therefore, there is no question whether the technology itself is a reason for our increasing concern about security in cyberspace, but the question should be posed how our policies will be able to set the appropriate mechanisms that would allow the fast innovation to be accompanied by required security measures.

ICT technology governance is a relatively new area. As with the dawn of first automobiles, planes or other technical innovations, people have started to use them without thinking too much on governance, safety or security. Actually, long before the safety belts were required, the autos were used for carrying military equipment, or used as basic construct for military machines. As with other technological innovations, autos and planes were used for demonstration of force for exploitation in conflict situation before there were proper rules how to use these machines safely in peacetime. Most technologies so far have found their use in defence industry, so it happens now with ICT technology. In addition to the military dimension of ICT technology usage, we are increasingly concerned about the exploitation of cyberspace for criminal purposes.

Profits of cybercriminal organisations are considered now exceeding the total revenue of drugs trafficking. Because of wide availability of computer technology exploitation expertise and relatively easy and low-cost access to cybercrime tools, this activity is expected to grow and will become a major source of revenue for organised crime. Symantec study reveals that 73 % of people in the U.S. have experienced some type of cybercrime [1]. Although it is difficult to attain realistic data on the extent of cybercrime, many companies are suffering from ransom attacks, spam and distributed denial of service attacks on daily basis. Europol as well as law enforcement agencies are trying to produce analyses that reflect the real magnitude of cybercrime but as companies are often hiding their security breaches and cyber intrusions, it is hard to present the real data on cybercrime in statistics [2]. The most common type of cybercrime is to spread malicious programmes through Internet that would hijack the personal computers of home users or of less-protected companies and will later form a botnet infrastructure for criminal industry.

This study will address the current challenges that policy-makers face in addressing the use of cyberspace for national security and criminal purposes, with a special focus on botnet infrastructure that could be exploited for both purposes. In addition to botnets, may other methods exist to disrupt, destruct or manipulate information in the computer systems. These methods are described in the other booklets of the current Springer cyber security series.

The paper will address the issue how to fight botnets from public policy perspective and will offer analysis and possible ways ahead for the policy-making community primarily. It will highlight the complex challenges of the misuse of ICT technologies, and will offer recommendations for policy-makers to guide possible public policy responses.

One of the key tasks that policymakers in cyber security will face in coming decades will be to bring the technology and policy aspects closer, and reach out to emerging markets and developing countries to address cyber threats at global level.

Therefore, this study will be another attempt among many that will aim to find the solutions for cyber security dilemma of our time. It will focus on strategic and organisational aspects while the twin study in this series will tackle the technology aspects of botnets, and will focus on technical measures of botnets' mitigation.

Section 2 of this study will describe the evolution of botnets into most common form of malicious cyber activity in today's Internet. It will serve as an introductory chapter that will describe the magnitude and complexity of the issue. It will also analyse the trends in botnets' development from mere nuisance towards serious revenue-creating criminal industry and towards an ascending strategic tool used in modern conflicts, and espionage.

Section 3 is devoted to the aspects of criminal use of the botnets. It will also describe the workings of cyber criminal industry, how botnets form a central backbone infrastructure for organised cybercrime and what are the trends in using botnets for cybercrime purposes.

Section 4 will discuss the use of botnets for political motivations. It will describe the use of botnets in espionage as well as in conflicts and political campaigns. Based on case studies of Georgia 2008 and Estonia 2007, the chapter will analyse how botnets could be used in the future conflicts.

Section 5 will discuss the policies and organisational countermeasures that are needed for increasing resilience of cyber assets at national level, including successful botnet mitigation. It will offer recommendations and best practices for national security decision-makers, law enforcement, and private sector in addressing cyber threats.

Section 6 will discuss international efforts in cyber security cooperation and how these efforts will support the disruption of criminal networks that run most of botnet infrastructures. It will describe what international initiatives have been implemented to fight with cyber threats, including the botnets, and will discuss the issue of capacity building in cyber security. It will offer also a glimpse into the legal difficulties surrounding the international fight with cybercrime and mitigation of botnets.

2 Botnets as a Global Challenge for Industry, Governments and Individual Computer Users

There are many methods how computer technology can be misused. One of the most successful technics used so far in malicious cyber activities is botnets, also called are robot networks of zombie computers. Botnet is a network of compromised computers, which are exploited without their owners realising that their computers are performing additional tasks. Botnets are used to collect sensitive information from governmental and commercial information systems, to steal personal data and identities, to distribute spam, and to launch denial of service attacks that flood the servers and might cause disruptions of online services. Botnets have facilitated probably a largest number of cyber criminal cases so far, and have been exploited for espionage purposes, for political campaigns and in recent conflicts.

Although a few analyses have outlined origins of the issue and offered possible mitigation strategies, general awareness stays low on the magnitude of political and economic consequences caused by botnets. Due to lack of reliable data, it is hard to assess the real magnitude of the problem. The varying numbers available on economic loss from cybercrime activities are resulting from general resistance of companies to reveal accurate data on security breaches, cybercrime incidents, and computer security failures. Governments also reveal only the tip of the iceberg on the magnitude of cyber espionage or intrusion incidents. Therefore, assessment of the real damage related to botnets is extremely difficult [3].

When looking at the significant cyber events in recent years, many politically motivated campaigns and other highly visible attacks have used botnets as a tool. However, these denial of service attacks that have attracted a great deal of media attention are not so numerous compared to covered espionage cases. Majority of significant cyber events are silent intrusions, where sensitive data are retrieved from compromised computers via some type of command and control server, a key element of botnets [4]. Therefore, elements of botnet infrastructure offer a significant enabling feature for most of serious cyber events.

There are following structural issues that need to be addressed when fighting botnets.

2.1 Botnets as an Awareness Issue

The major reason why it is possible to use the hijacked personal computers for cybercrime and for other malicious purposes, lies in the fact that an average computer user is unaware on the threats in the Internet. As long as understanding about safe use of computer technology is limited at individual level, botnets will stay as an unfortunate by-product of our digital societies.

Although some special botnets exist that are created by governments for concrete operations, and are not even partly owned by average computer users, the majority of bots in criminal botnets belong to innocent average users.

Awareness of end-users, and owners of corporate and public information systems could be much higher. Cyber security as a shared responsibility where individual users also have a role, is repeated in many national cyber security strategies. There are few good practices how governments have launched awareness campaigns among larger public, or how private and public sector have cooperated on educating computer users, but more efforts are needed to achieve progress in this field [5].

At the same time, due to increasing sophistication of malware, individual computer users need assistance either from governmental computer security agencies or private sector. In some OECD countries there are excellent examples of responsible corporate behavior of ISPs in warning users and removing botnet malware from the networks at an early stage [6].

2.2 Botnets as a Legal and Organisational Issue

Successful fight with botnets presupposes there are few legal and organisational elements in place. The first is the existence of appropriate legal framework that allows the law enforcement authorities to operate effectively in dismantling the botnet infrastructure, and facilitates the judicial authorities to prosecute the wrong-doers. The second element is a cooperation mechanism between law enforcement and private sector, specially Internet Service Providers (ISP). The third element that has a central role in botnet mitigation cases consists of international cooperation in cross-border botnet investigation. Often the investigation will reach to more than one country, and therefore, timely reaction will depend on both the law enforcement capacity and on legal system of other countries. Although more than 50 countries have acceded the only existing international legal instrument, the Council of Europe Convention of Cybercrime, that aims at offering minimum requirements for national laws in fighting cybercrime and in executing joint international investigations, great disparity still exists in national legal systems both in Europe and worldwide [7].

The key issue relates to general capacity to form a timely information sharing and early warning system between private and public sector that would share threat intelligence on botnets, and will facilitate cleaning up the networks. Evidence suggests that there is no uniform performance of private companies in sharing information, and avoiding misuse of their networks. The most critical link in the Internet infrastructure, the Internet Service Providers, are very rarely mandated by the governments to assume greater responsibility in providing more reliable infrastructure for information society services. Private sector efforts in keeping their networks relatively clean from malware are currently observed in few OECD countries, specially in Japan and Finland, and this voluntary cooperation approach would provide a model for the public authorities in other advanced countries how to address the issue of botnets [8]. However, more and more cyber security experts suggest that instead of voluntary and self-regulatory cooperation models a proper regulatory policy for Internet Service Providers should be developed that will mandate private sector companies to take timely measures against malware in their networks.

2.3 Botnets as a Side-Effect of Fast-Growing Internet Economy

The organisations that provide Internet connections, i.e. Internet Service Providers (ISP), network providers, hosting providers, webmail providers and other owners of large information systems, control the communications and Internet infrastructure.

Among these organisations, the majority are privately owned ISPs, or hosting companies, routinely trafficking real data in Internet. Logically, the responsibility to monitor, localise and neutralise botnets, or other malware, lies with these companies. However, the situation is quite complex in reality. There are many categories of different companies in this industry. First, there are retail Internet providers operating with very small margins and cannot afford good security practices. Secondly, there are large companies with huge amounts of traffic where awareness on security issues is low, and countermeasures are not applied to keep networks clean. Research suggests that although there are plenty of recommendations available to achieve better security awareness and botnet mitigation among ISPs, not all companies follow these guidelines. And finally, there is an increasing number of rouge ISPs or hosts whose business model is primarily to provide necessary infrastructure for malicious network activity, ranging from sending spam to conducting serious organised criminal activities (distributing child pornography, hosting botnet command and control servers, engaging in online extortion etc.) [9]. Botnets usually reside in the networks of all these three categories of companies, many of them unaware that a portion of their activity is aimed at aiding criminal activity against companies in other economic sectors.

Many other economic sectors are suffering from the lack of awareness and good security that should be provided by the ISPs and network companies. Banking sector is allegedly suffering huge losses a year to various forms of cybercrime. Increasingly, the utility companies in energy, gas and water sectors are subject to botnets attacks with an aim of extortion. And finally, the mid- and small sized businesses relying on online services will suffer, as their business model is built on Internet as a critical infrastructure, but they lack necessary resources to offer safe financial transactions for their customers.

The paradox is that widespread activity that brings revenue to Internet and the telecommunications sector is consequently reaping the revenue from other economic sectors. It leads to an inevitable conclusion that a proper public policy response should be considered in order to curtail this trend. In this context, governments seem to consider whether tougher regulatory approach is needed since the market self-regulation has not brought desired effects. The debate is going on what kind of regulation is needed to address the issue effectively without loosing the competitiveness of the Internet service sector [10].

2.4 Botnets as a Global Cooperation Issue

There is a clear trend on the rise that botnet activity moves away from advanced economies and will gain new heights in emerging markets, where the number of computer and mobile telephone users increases rapidly [11]. As the ICT represents a great equaliser and enabler of all other economic activities in emerging markets and developing countries, we can expect the rapid spread of Internet services also to the poorer regions in the world. Alongside with positive effects it will unfortunately also mean that the number of botnets will grow that originate from emerging markets and developing countries. Given the experience in the Western countries where it has taken decades to raise awareness on security issues of ICT development, and where the law enforcement is still struggling to fund its high tech crime operations, we can expect that cyber security measures in the emerging and developing countries will take even more time and effort to build.

Advanced countries have realised the global challenge of cyber threats and have already started to launch necessary policies to respond to this. But they themselves are still in the phase of advancing necessary organisational and technical capabilities to fight with cybercrime and tackle cyber security problems on their own territories. Therefore, there is still limited manpower and resources available to reach outside the developed world. There are few policies starting now to help emerging markets in this uphill struggle, but in order to tackle the issue effectively, we need serious efforts at global level. Ignoring cyber security challenges in the developing world will cost the advanced countries as well as the emerging and developing countries in the long run.

One of the great challenges in coming decades will be to prevent global cyberspace becoming even more contaminated by botnets and other types of malware. For successful prevention, realistic assessment is needed how many computers worldwide in which regions are potentially being commanded by some malicious programme or how contaminated country's networks are. One can use different metrics for this kind of assessment. In order to analyse from where botnets could originate in the future, we should look at several statistical factors. The first will be the number of computer users in the country. The general wisdom goes that countries with a higher number of end-users will also rank highly in botnets, or in other types of malware. In the background of ICT revolution in the emerging markets, we can expect new countries entering to the lists of botnet activity after the Western countries have implemented policies to achieve cleaner networks.

The second measurement method will include the existence and efficiency of governance structures for addressing cyber threats in a country. This includes technical and organisational preparedness for incident response, mostly the existence of national cyber security and incident response authority as well as cybercrime or high tech crime unit and necessary public–private partnership mechanisms to facilitate botnet mitigation. This preparedness includes also judicial and criminal justice framework as well as maturity of cooperation and coordination structures between different cyber security stakeholders in a country. Governance structures will be efficient if there is a reasonable degree of technical know-how, organisational capacity and supporting policy mechanisms that will contribute to the resilience of information systems and networks in a country. The weaker these governance structures are, the more difficult it will be to tackle the cyber threats, including botnets.

Abovementioned elements of national preparedness are still being harmonised in the European Union, in the U.S., Canada, Australia and in other technologically advanced countries. Creating the same framework globally will require substantial efforts in coming decades.

3 Botnets and Cybercrime

Cybercriminal industry has flourished due to relatively low cost and high efficiency of using botnets as a major method to gain criminal profits. The criminal
botnet market has evolved from amateur botnet infrastructure into a highly organised criminal industry where it will be possible to rent out botnets for a certain
purpose, to get quality guarantee and also customer service.

The major criminal activities for which botnets are used is the distribution of
spam e-mails, stealing bank credentials and identities for attacking financial services, using Distributed Denial of Service attacks for extortion, gaining criminal
profits through simulating false response to advertising, infecting computers via
websites and other similar activities.

The majority of most sophisticated botnets have been built for attacking financial sector, and big companies in this sector are probably the most experienced
organisations in state-of-art cyber defence technics [12]. Governments have been
struggling in preventing the threat and responding to widespread issue of the botnets, placing emphasis on national public–private partnership to address the issue
at the highest level [13]. Effective fight with criminal botnet infrastructure should
involve many industries and has a strong international component due to cyber
criminal organisations operating in different jurisdictions simultaneously. Solving
a cybercrime case requires substantative collaboration efforts, posing so a complex
international and legal cooperation issue that involves a large number of public
and private sector players in many countries.

3.1 Botnets Attacking Financial Services

Financial services are traditionally the most common target of criminal botnets.
Older botnets designed for banks, such as Black Energy and Darkness have
reaped profits from banking sector in the Western Europe and the US since 2007.
The most common botnet specialising on banking is a Zeus botnet that is alleged
to cost the US banks as much as 10$ Million during last 5 years [14]. All these
"mainstream banking botnets" have their roots in the Russian Business Network,
a cyber criminal network that has operated as a legal Internet service provider up
to 2007, went underground in 2007, and has since distributed its cells worldwide
[15]. Some of these criminal banking-botnets have been also used for other lines
of business, such as attacking the EU carbon trading market [16]. Although the
Zeus botnet is being mitigated by large international collective action initiated
by Microsoft, it still exists. Newer and more advanced botnets might emerge
soon.

More sophisticated botnets already have started to emerge that attack banking
sector. These are stealthier against intrusion detection and bypass conventional infection identifications. In May 2012, a Jericho botnet was discovered with origins on

two continents. It represents an example of how criminal organisations are engaged in issuing ever-improving malware in order to gain criminal profits [17].

3.2 Spam Providing Botnets

A famous case dating back to 2008 was a take-down of online spam servers' hosting company McColo Corp. in Califonia. It was one of the leading players in the so-called "bulletproof hosting" market that operated in the shadow of bigger ISPs. McColo was responsible for two thirds of global spam market and was a host for many botnets' command and control servers. The takedown was a common effort of security research community and law enforcement [18]. The number of these kind of 100 % malicious hosting companies that allow servers to remain online regardless of complaints has been diminishing since then as the cybercriminal market is more devided by now. But criminal profits gained through this kind of activity are too big for cyber crime gangs just vanishing. Rather, they will retreat to the territories with less stringent judicial powers and weaker law enforcement, or apply more sophisticated methods to avoid early detection.

A good case study how control servers for botnets are switched, and criminal activity is restored, is a Rustock botnet which was hosted by McColo until 2008. Rustock run from 2006 to 2011 comprising up to 2, 4 millions of infected computers and was sending spam with selling unlicensed or fake pharmaceuticals. After McColo takedown in 2008, Rustock control servers emerged again in Russia, and later in the U.S., with spam levels restored by 2009. The botnet industry was cleverly distributed to smaller ISPs to avoid attention, but proved to be very resistant to take-down efforts [19]. Microsoft finally initiated a major collaborative effort to dismantle the Rustock botnet that sent millions of spam e-mails a day selling potentially dangerous fake drugs [20].

Another spam botnet, called Bredolab, existed successfully for 4 years sending e-mails that infected individual computers through legitimate websites, and built up a zombie network for other criminal activities. Bredolab was also used for identity theft through social networks, such as Facebook. Many of its control servers operated in large Dutch ISPs. In 2010–2011, the Dutch authorities disabled 143 command and control servers in order to take it down. A Russian citizen operating in Armenia was arrested for masterminding the botnet [21].

A recent case of large spam botnet takedown includes Grum case. Grum botnet was a good example how global botnet infrastructure has moved out from Europe and from the U.S. to other areas. Grum had control servers located in Panama, Russia and Ukraine. Once servers were taken down in Panama, they re-emerged in Russia. After taking down Russian control servers, activity switched to Ukraine, which is believed to be one of the safe havens for control servers and bot herders [22]. There are many other countries where states do not regard cybercrime as their major responsibility, and where mitigation of botnets is next to impossible.

3.3 Extortion DDOS Attacks Against E-commerce and Critical Companies

High end cybercrime activity and extortion attacks towards critical infrastructure will be the next serious attack vector after current massive botnet infrastructure will be mitigated by collective efforts. More resistant P-2-P botnets will emerge and other malicious activities will be used against critical companies and e-commerce.

Many security researchers and national security analysts are very worried on accessibility and ease of serious cyber attacks carried out towards national critical infrastructure. The recent spear-phishing attack towards U.S. gas pipelines is just one of disclosed attack attempts made by unknown groups of hackers [23].

Researchers in McAfee state that majority of personnel in critical U.S. utilities is not concerned about security making these companies vulnerable for possible extortion attacks. Regular cyber extortion attempts are made towards many critical utilities already now [24].

Systematic efforts are made in many countries to help the companies to ward off attacks against critical companies. In the UK, a governmental cyber agency will help the private sector to monitor network traffic and take necessary measures if air traffic, energy sector or telecom companies will be affected [25]. DDOS attacks already have hit critical companies in the UK, with an aim to blackmail large sums [26].

The trend of rouge proxy actors and criminal groups merging in malicious cyber activity is on the rise. In the U.S., Coreflood botnet was recently discovered that was used mainly criminal purposes against the U.S. companies, but may have also executed few espionage tasks of stealing secrets from government agencies and defence contractors [27].

3.4 Conficker

Conficker represents a mysterious botnet that spread very quickly, but it is less known for what motivations it was actually created. It was used in criminal activity, but given the high publicity of the virus, it also served as an awareness raising incident for companies and governments.

Estimates of the number of computers infected in its peak reach up to 7 million computers worldwide. It tried to exploit vulnerability on Windows XP related systems and had many advanced features, such as blocking access to security websites and using encryption for its payload channels [28].

Conficker spread also to several sensitive governmental systems, such as the U.K. Ministry of Defence, Royal Navy warships and submarines. It also affected information systems in Bundeswehr and in the French military [29].

Microsoft was acting swiftly to launch a technology industry collaboration to mitigate consequences of Conficker. Organizations in this effort included Microsoft,

Afilias, ICANN, Neustar, Verisign, CNNIC, Public Internet Registry, Global Domains International, Inc., M1D Global, AOL, Symantec, F-Secure, ISC, researchers from Georgia Tech, The Shadowserver Foundation, Arbor Networks and Support Intelligence.

3.5 Patterns of Botnet Activity Moving Outside Europe and the U.S

After takedown of the Bredolab and Rustock, the number of infected US computers has decreased and the country is no longer considered one of the leading distributors of spam. Numbers of European countries as top spam sources are diminishing too, replaced by those located on the Asian and South American continent.

Considering the fact that the size of botnets changes all the time, and that there are smaller botnets in every country active in spending spam, a number of new countries have emerged in spam distribution. They include India, Brazil, China, Ukraine, Indonesia, Taiwan, Vietnam and Russia.

There might be an emerging trend that as botnets can be commanded from anywhere in the world, the bot herders will decide to concentrate their infection efforts on countries that still don't have effective laws addressing cybercrime. Additionally, another logical step for them is to spread botnets throughout various countries. In case that one of the control servers will be taken down, they can switch herding activity to other territories.[1] The trend of new mobile device botnets being formed in emerging markets is specially sobering after recent successful collaborative efforts in the Western countries to neutralise the large botnets [30].

3.6 Botnets in Mobile Devices

One of the rising trends is a security challenge presented by the mobile devices. Mobile devices do not receive regular patches, but rely increasingly on browsers [31]. Therefore, mobile equipment presents a new vector for malicious cyber activity, including formation of new large botnets.

Specially exposed are small and medium businesses, which are open to high severity vulnerabilities from the increasing levels of mobile devices used to access and download company data. IT security managers in smaller companies cannot keep up with the rate of discovery of severe vulnerabilities these devices bring to their corporate network and they lack a standardized approach to mitigate the risks from different types of mobile devices. Even though they feel exposed to mobile device security risk, smaller businesses do not feel they have adequate tools to assess

---

[1] See the Grum botnet case in earlier section, for instance.

and mitigate these risks as they do with laptops, desktops and servers. Company data is at risk of being leaked off the device and company servers are at risk of being attacked by mobile devices [32].

4 Botnets and National Security

National security analysts are worried when witnessing an ever increasing growth of cyber intrusions into critical public and private information systems, and denial of service attacks. Defence and security authorities in most of the countries try to predict what would be the possible impact of exploiting cyber tools in future conflicts. Although a full-scale cyberwar is still difficult to imagine, we can predict some dynamics in future conflicts when analysing recent politically motivated cyber attacks.

In a nutshell, the analysis below will show that cyber tools will be used in future conflicts as a method to achieve certain political aims alongside with other methods. It will be less likely to witness cyber conflicts that occur only in the electronic domain. Inter-state conflicts still occur for political reasons, so will serious state sponsored cyber attacks. In the future, more sophisticated tools can be used in these occasions.

However, there is no trend of increasing number in political conflicts because of widely available cyber attack technology. Rather, majority of cyber incidents are related to criminal or espionage activities. For this reason, national security analysts should be aware on the probability of cyber methods used as a part of future conflicts, but should not overestimate the probability of serious inter-state conflicts occurring in cyber domain. Therefore, instead of going along with a current hype of cyber offense that is fuelled by certain industrial interests, more attention should be turned to raising overall resilience of national critical information systems, both in public and private sector.

At present, a major concern for national security decision-makers is widespread cyber espionage that systematically retrieves sensitive government information and industrial intellectual property from the Western nations. It is very difficult to measure the exact loss that cyber espionage presents, and it is equally difficult to draw conclusions how the trend of loosing significant information through cyber tools is weakening the Western industrial power in long term. But it is clear that most revenue providing companies are being closely followed by different cyber groups, whether for espionage or crime purposes. There are fears that continued espionage against the West will ultimately change the power distribution in the current international system.

Many espionage operations use the command and control servers that are similar to botnet control servers. Massive espionage cases have reached nearly every industry and sector, as well as governmental networks. Botnets that facilitate espionage function similarly to those botnets retrieving personal data and bank account credentials. Computers send information to C&C servers that are carefully disguised in order to avoid attribution. Nevertheless, analysts can usually draw quite accurate conclusions when looking at the list of targets, at timing of intrusions, or at other indirect evidence that usually allows to determine which perpetrators might be interested in specific information stolen.

4.1 Cyber Espionage Against Governments and Companies

Exponential network and technological advances enabling witting and unwitting massive cybered transfers of wealth out of Western nations, however, have made cyberspace into a conflict space. Rather than the benign mutually governed international commerce arena envisioned by its early advocates, cyberspace has facilitated asymmetric strategic game-changing properties for the international system [33].

The penetrations to classified and unclassified military networks in late 90s gave the hints of what the future of cyber era would look like. An incident called Moonlight Maze was the first massive intrusion attack towards computer systems at the Pentagon, NASA, Energy Department, private universities, and research laboratories. When the intrusion was discovered in 2000, it had already had been going on for nearly 2 years. Before the discovery, the intruders were able to view tens of thousands of files, among them maps of military installations, troop configurations and military hardware designs. Investigation traced the trail back to a mainframe computer in the former Soviet Union but the sponsor of the attacks is unknown and Russia denied any involvement.

Even more sophisticated massive cyberespionage incident code named Titan Rain begun in 2004, when hackers could find vulnerabilities in the U.S. military computers and retrieve sensitive data [34]. The anonymity of cyber espionage and search for the identity of the attackers posed a challenge. Investigation could trace attacks to computers in China, which did not present the clear evidence, but circumstantial proof that some Chinese entities were involved in this incident. Most of sensitive investigation data on this case is classified, but few open source analysts have hinted the possible link between the Chinese mafia cybercrime triads and government [35].

A less known but equally serious incident occurred in the U.S. where the municipal officials in Mountain View, California noticed unusal Internet traffic viewing the local maps. It was appearently linked to the terrorist activity trying to collect data on infrastructure facilities in the U.S.

In last years, regular espionage cases are reported in the U.S. media on Chinese hackers stealing the industrial secrets, the layouts of factories and other sensitive data of companies [36].

Compared to huge cybercrime botnets, cyber espionage botnets present a differently designed infrastructure. There is more time spent on technical misdirection in order to loose traces, the number of infected computers as well as C&C servers is smaller. The espionage botnets are built to run smaller targeted information retrieving operations compared to criminal botnets where millions of hijacked computers are used. Spy networks also use targeted e-mails, or spear-phishing for distributing malware. Therefore, there is more human element involved than in automated cybercrime botnets. Increasing cyber espionage malware suggests that the complexity and scope of spying activities in networks will only increase in the future. Detection of this kind of malware is extremely difficult and beyond the ability of common anti-virus programmes. Spying malware also obfuscates the stolen data in order to bypass the common intrusion detection technics.

There are few espionage examples that show the magnitude of the threat and increasing technical sophistication level that governments, companies and even non-governmental organisations face.

4.1.1 Ghostnet

One of the largest known espionage cases involved over 1295 computers in 103 countries, and one third of them were sensitive information systems of the government's diplomatic services, NGO-s, international organisations and news media.

Ghostnet, when it became known in 2009, was one of the most sophisticated methods seen so far. A Trojan called Gh0st RAT was able to take a full real-time control of infected machines, look for specific information in files, and using web cameras and microphones for espionage activities. Its command and control servers were tracked to many geographic locations, including commercial servers in Hainan island in China [37].

Malicious Tibetan-themed email campaigns were targeting pro-Tibetan organizations and making them install malware on their machines. Gh0st RAT C&C servers have been spotted a number of times in conjunction with similar attacks.

4.1.2 Aurora

A series of new attack trends has emerged where the government sponsored entities have acted against global companies registered in the U.S. In 2010, Google became a subject of a sophisticated and targeted cyber attack, which resulted in significant loss of data. The attacks were aimed at retrieving information on Chinese human rights activists. After the incident, Google threatened to withdraw from Chinese market.

This incident showed that highly sophisticated attack methods that so far have been targeting mostly governmental information systems, can be used also towards a commercial company [38]. Internet Explorer vulnerability that was exploited in the penetration, has been also used simultaneously against Adobe's and numerous other companies' networks.

4.1.3 ShadyRAT

In 2011, a Remote Access Tool was discovered by McAfee that is named Shady RAT by security researchers. This tool has infiltrated networks in the U.S.

government, defence contractors, in Canadian government, in a number of Asian nations and in the International Olympics Committee. The espionage operation is alleged to originate from a nation state, and its beginning dates back to 2006. The list of government agencies, NGOs and few companies as targets, which are located in the US, in Canada, in Korea, in Singapore, in Taiwan and in Indonesia offers circumstantial evidence that this operation was planned and executed by a country, not by a criminal organisation [39].

4.2 Botnets Used in Active Political Campaigns or in Conflicts

Among the most significant cyber events in last 6 years, roughly one third of them are politically motivated [40]. This shows that preventing and mitigating botnets, and dismantling their command and control infrastructure serves also the purposes of national security.

The major reason for using botnets for politically motivated campaigns as a tool lies in their non-attributable efficiency. Similar to espionage and criminal activity, bots are anonymous digital soldiers that can be sent to fulfil a political mission without large costs and with no exact indication who is behind them. At the same time, they can achieve temporary and highly visible effects of governmental websites not responding, information not being available or vital online services being disrupted for some time in a country. Sometimes these effects are desirable in the larger political context, and then the use of botnets will benefit the masterminds who want to coerce their old political challengers with new modern tools.

On 4 July 2009, thousands of private and governmental websites in the U.S. and in South Korea became victims to a large DDOS attack. As always with botnets attacks, they originated technically from many different countries. But post-incident analysis pointed to North Korea as a possible culprit [41].

The Internet services and servers in the West Bank and Gaza were taken down by DDOS attacks in 2011 as a reaction of UNICEF adopting Palestine to become a member of the organisation. This has allegedly raised enough anger in Israel, and again, DDOS attacks proved to be an effective and visible way to demonstrate political disagreement [42]. This case supports the overall argument presented in this chapter that serious politically motivated cyber attacks will serve just as an extention of the existing conflicts between nations in cyberspace.

Cyber attacks are seen by nations as one tool among many that could be used for political purposes. Therefore, it will be not such a challenge to guess who is behind certain activities if the cyber attacks are analysed in historic and political context.

Two case studies below indicate how cyber operations can support conflicts or political campaigns, these are Estonia 2007 and Georgia 2008 cyber attacks against online private sector services and governmental websites. They will offer a glimpse of how the similar future conflicts would look like and how cyber tools will be used for political coercion purposes.

4.3 Case Study of Estonia: Botnets Facilitating Digital Siege of a Country

In April 2007, Estonia relocated the Soviet war memorial from the central part of the city to the military cemetery. This triggered a massive political campaign with riots in the streets, diplomatic disputes, physical siege of the Estonian Embassy in Moscow and also large-scale cyber attacks. The case study below will show that cyber attacks were used as just one tool among many in a larger campaign, and therefore, it will offer a lesson how cyber attacks could be used in similar future operations.

The political campaign against Estonia, triggered by the relocation of the Second World War monument, had many unconventional features, including first large-scale cyber attacks organised against an entire country. The other elements of this campaign—coordinated mass riots, well-financed foreign propaganda, Kremlin-associated youth groups attacking Estonian and the EU embassies in Moscow, economic sanctions etc. manifested the new type of "foreign influence". In this new reality the campaign was taking place not only in "material" world, but mostly in the "cognitive realm" as it was largely carried out in the mass media and exploited the mass media to prepare for the campaign. The streets riots could be triggered because of disseminating the false news in the Russian-speaking mass media. The world media was flooded about the dubious news on relocation of the monument, sometime saying that this was destroyed not relocated. The ability of strategic communication by the Estonian authorities was hampered and online news outlets were disrupted by DDOS attacks etc.

The Bronze Soldier, a Soviet war monument in Tallinn, became a major element in the build-up of the political campaign in April 2007. The monument has been standing in the center of Tallinn since 1947. The Bronze Soldier would probably still stand there if the victory in the Second World War would not have become an increasingly important element in the revived Russian nationalism in the beginning of a new Millennia. Glorifying the Victory day in Russia affected also the ethnic Russians living outside the Russian Federation. As most ethnic Russians in Estonia rely for their daily news on the Russian media channels, their perception of the world reflects the reality that the state-controlled Russian media is portraying. With the help of these media channels, the local ethnic Russians were part of the information field where the victory in the Second World War was seen as a Soviet achievement, and where the ordinary Russians are portrayed as major martyrs of the war. In fact, in the old Soviet history books, the role of the Western countries in fighting Nazi regime was not too strongly emphasised and the majority of the Soviet population believed that the Soviet Union was the sole dominant player in achieving the defeat of Hitler. For many, victory in the war served as a major factor legitimising the existence of the Soviet Union.

In the Baltic states, the reading of history was always different. In the 1990s the democratic Russian elites recognised the fact-based history and Soviet annexation of the Baltic states. The historic fact of the existing secret protocols of the Molotov-Rippentrop Pact that devided Romania, Poland, the Baltic states and Finland into territorial spheres of influence between Nazi Germany and Soviet Russia, was widely recognized in the Jeltsin era Russia. But this fact was not too often mentioned in the mainstream media channels in Russia after 2000. Since the return of Soviet narratives and symbolics in Russia, defeat of Nazis and "liberation" of Baltic states also served as a legitimisation argument for Soviet occupation in the Baltic states in 1945–1991. Also many other historic events were treated with a great deal of creativity to make them suit the glorification of Soviet victory in the Second World War.

4.3.1 Bronze Night, Riots and Political Pressure

Estonian authorities had initially planned to remove the Bronze soldier after the 9 May celebration in 2007. But the preparations for the exhumation and identification of buried soldiers next to the monument have been planned for April. The monument area was separated and access limited in mid-April 2007. On 26 April a tent was built in the monument area to facilitate the exhumation of buried soldiers. Several developments led to the mass demonstration at the monument site in the same night, among them calls in Russian speaking Internet chat rooms that the monument will be demolished. The violent riots started in the evening of 26 April, which resulted the major streets of Tallinn smashed and shops looted. The police could restore the order, and arrest many rioters by early morning of 27 April. The government emergency meeting was held during the night and it was decided to relocate the monument to the Defence Forces' cemetery in the early morning of 27 April. The reactions to unexpected relocation prompted a political pressure, siege of the Estonian embassy in Moscow by the Kremlin-associated youth organisation Nashi, and undeclared economic sanctions. As a reconciliation measure agreed between the head of the EU Presidency Angela Merkel and Russian leader Putin, a Duma delegation was sent to Tallinn to negotiate a solution with the Estonian side. Before the Duma delegation arrived to Tallinn, it demanded publicly that the democratically elected Estonian government should step down [43].

Cyber attacks took place after all these major events on 26–28 April had started, and lasted three weeks until 18 May. There were other elements of the campaign happening in Estonia. The riots broke out not only in Tallinn on 26–27 April, but also in other cities, mostly in Russian speaking smaller cities. Among other methods used, some of them were also directed against public order, such as a campaign of cars driving slowly and signalling in the center of the city for a day. Most of these events were accompanied by heavy media campaign in Russian speaking news media against Estonia in order to mount political pressure on the government [44]. As cyber attacks had limited the possibility of the Estonian media outlets to spread the news, the perception of the country being cut off from the Internet was created. It took some time before the leading Western media channels were able to cover the news on the ground and able to find out what really happened to the soldier monument.

4.3.2 Three Waves of Cyber Attacks

Attacks involved different actors with different skills level during the 3 week period of siege on the country's online services. In the initial phase most active group was a large wave of hacktivists, where people with limited technical skills were following the instructions on certain websites, and acted according to these guidelines. As the early relocation of the monument was a surprise, the first wave of cyber attacks was a relatively simple denial of service and defacement attacks, meant to disrupt the Internet availability and disable websites.

Much more professional and coordinated attacks were following in two other waves in May, when serious Distributed Denial of Service (DDOS) attacks targeted the online banking, the Internet Service Providers and other civilian critical infrastructures [45]. For most of these attacks, the resources and pre-coordination was necessary as they involved large botnets that are usually costly and should be rented from the criminal groups in advance. The main attack with rented criminal botnets started on 8 May at 11 pm, which was the first hour of 9 May by Moscow time, the Victory day in the WWII. Large botnets started to target Estonian servers that consisted of millions hijacked computers [46]. These kind of botnets cost quite a bit of money and are usually exploited by the organised cyber criminal groups. Some of the attacks were carried out in waves and were executed with very precise timing. Some of them were well-coordinated and required resources unavailable to common people. Some of the attacks could have been fatal and cause even more serious damage to the country's critical information infrastructure if application of the rapid countermeasures had failed. In later stages there was also involvement of more skilled actors who had prior experience in launching different sophisticated cyber aggressions in addition to DDOS attacks.

A large scale botnet attack looks like the river is hundreds times bigger suddenly, i.e. the floods of data disrupt your communication services. As a last resort, one of the mitigation strategies of IT security experts was to limit the Internet connectivity with outside world in order to allow the Internet services run inside Estonia. At the peak of the attacks, the Internet connection was limited for few days. During these days it was impossible to reach Estonia via Internet from outside world. At the time of heavy political campaign, with riots in the streets and propaganda attacks against Estonia over relocation of the World War II monument, disconnection from Internet added confusion as to what really happens in the country.

The decision to limit connectivity was necessary in order to restore the online services inside Estonia and avoid chaos and psychological pressure on people. But the outside world interpreted this as total disruption, and the news were spreading that Estonia was cut off from Internet as a result of cyber attacks. Considering the need to restore normal way of life that includes using high number of online services every day in Estonia, this last resort was justified, even when looked in retrospective.[2] Economic effects of the cyber attacks were never published as companies regarded politically motivated cyber attacks as force majeur. The estimated cost for one bank during the siege of 3 weeks was ca 200 million Estonian

---

[2] Although Estonia did limit Internet connectivity at the peak of attacks on 8–9 May, the connection was never cut off entirely, and Internet always worked inside Estonia. The Internet architecture in Estonia allows to limit connectivity to outside world and maintain functionality of online services inside the country. In order to allow Estonian citizens to conduct their everyday online business, the method of limiting connectivity with the rest of the world was used as a last resort for few days during the cyber attacks.

kroons. And there were many banks, ISPs and other companies under attack. However, a major economic defeat came later, with trade volumes stopping transit through Estonia as a punishment for relocating the Bronze soldier.

Estonia as a small, modern, technology-savvy country was an ideal test-ground for cyber attacks with political motivations. The number of online services offered by private and public entities in Estonia is high. For instance, 98 % of the banking sector relies on electronic communications, over 90 % people submit their tax declarations online, and government agencies use a unique e-government information system to do their daily business. Estonia's personal identification management system, which is based on electronic ID cards, facilitates many transactions between citizens and the state, as well as with private companies. Such high penetration of online services contributes to smoother administration and allows the country to cut down on transaction costs in the economy. But as witnessed in 2007, this system had also weaknesses that make the whole society vulnerable to computer network attacks.

Botnet attacks proved to be a useful tool to reach the strategic goal of an entire operation—to disrupt online services in the country, coerce its citizens and discredit it in the eyes of the world. Flooding attacks are handy method in these kind of campaigns for many reasons. First, the DDOS attacks are effective and cost-efficient method in order to temporarily cut the ability of the government to communicate the real events on the ground, allowing so to feed different information to world's media. Secondly, cyber attacks against the civilian infrastructure, i.e. online services, financial institutions, and others, could be organised with an aim to disrupt routine life of population and shake the confidence of people. At the same time, they did not cause major physical damage that could be treated as the act of violence, and would fall under the existing international law provisions that cover the use of force. Attacks stayed in the grey zone where no international laws apply so far. Thirdly, coordinated large-scale cyber attacks were probably meant also to serve as a show-off to other countries in Europe, and elsewhere. The U.S., for instance, has allocated 30 billion USD for governmental cyber security in 2008, following the Estonian cyber attacks and other similar developments in cyberspace [47].

4.3.3 Lessons Learned

When someone asks for a single most important lesson from the Estonian cyber attacks, it would undoubtedly be the need for more advanced international cooperation in cyber security. At the moment when 400 times more data are flooding your servers from all the countries in the world, the mitigation can be carried out only with the help of international contacts and networks. That's what has saved Estonia in 2007 from the worse. The Estonian Computer Emergency Response Team (CERT) contacted other CERTs, which, together with international informal information security networks, helped to neutralise the distributed denial of service attacks. At the same time, the Estonian information security specialists mitigated the attacks for 3 weeks on 24/7 basis to enable online services to run in Estonia. With the help of law enforcement, CERTs, and ISPs cooperating in ca

100 countries, and with assistance of international informal IT security professional networks, Estonia was able to mitigate the attacks. No formal intergovernmental cyber crises mechanism existed in 2007, but there was a large informal network present that helped to cut off botnets in many countries.

Another major conclusion of Estonian 2007 events was of strategic nature. Cyber siege showed that there is a new type of powerful asymmetric attack method that could be used in any future conflicts. This method allows to influence the developments in other countries and regions from a great distance and remain anonymous. As real-time attribution of cyber attacks is still difficult, cyber tools can create the necessary effect without taking the political responsibility. Organising a large-scale cyberattack against a country that depends on online services is an efficient tool to achieve political goals of intimidation and disruption.

There are a few other strategic implications that could be drawn from this experience. First, international society has reached a point where the technological race has outpaced its collective ability to provide efficient policies and crises response mechanisms for global telecommunication infrastructure and the Internet. As Estonian mitigation case has showed, in 2007 the world lacked formal and institutional cyber alert mechanisms and response systems for managing large-scale cyber incidents. The second important implication was that after the Estonian attacks the issue of cyber security got elevated to national security issue in many advanced countries that are depending on information infrastructure. It prompted the first NATO Cyber Defence Policy in 2008 and made sure that cyber security has finally left a corner in IT departments', brought to centre stage, and bolstered with political attention. Most advanced countries started actively build resilience of national cyber assets, and engage in international cyber security cooperation.

After the Bronze Soldier event in 2007, Estonian Internet traffic resumed to normal levels and has stayed like this ever since. In order to investigate cyber attacks, Estonia turned to over 50 countries requesting cooperation in criminal investigation and in extradition of cybercriminals related to organising cyber attacks. Only one country did not respond positively to a criminal investigation request.[3]

4.4 Georgia 2008: Cyber Attacks Facilitating Strategic Goals in Kinetic War

The Georgian attacks were the first cyber attacks that occurred during the military conflict, being in that matter the subject to international law.[4] Cyber attacks were launched

---

[3] International law enforcement cooperation was very good during and after the event, only one country, which has also not joined a major international cyber convention, the Council of Europe Convention for Cybercrime, declined the international obligation under the Mutual Legal Assistance Treaty to investigate the cyber attacks organised from its territory.

[4] The Law of Armed Conflicts and International Humanitarian Law regulate when the use of force in armed conflicts has occured and which principles apply when using the force.

before the military activity started on the disputed territory of South Ossetia, with a possible strategic aim to cut the ability of Georgian government to communicate with their citizens and with the world. The open source analyses on Georgian cyber attacks and military invasion point to a close coordination between the two processes [48].

The attacks started with defacement campaign of the president Shaakasvili website, as well as with the Distributed Denial of Service attacks on other government ministries' websites. Although the attackers were predominantly anonymous civilians and some criminals from notorious Russian Business Network, there was also an involvement of servers of the state controlled telecommunications companies that helped to reroute the Georgian Internet traffic [49]. As the attacks were carried out by hackers recruited for this purpose earlier, there was no need for military involvement in these attacks. The organisers of the attacks were aware of the Russian military movements in advance, and they synchronised the attacks during the conflict as necessary. Many of the attack methods and difficult operational tasks were launched suddenly, suggesting the preparation had been carried out earlier for using these methods. The social networks were used to recruit the civilian hackers, with an involvement of criminal networks as some of the servers used in attacks were known to belong to Russian cybercrime circles.

In Georgia, the attack technics used were similar, but have elevated to a higher technical sophistication level compared to Estonian attacks. The SQL injections, and HTTP-based attack tools proved to be more efficient in this attack than ICMP attacks in Estonia. Also, the defacement contents of the Georgian websites had been prepared well in advance.

The Georgian attacks were widely analysed by the information security community and most of the traces were quite clearly leading to Russian criminal networks. How the synchronization occurred with military advances, remains unclear. But the attacks served their purpose well in creating chaos and uncertainty in Georgian government, and disrupting the ability to communicate their messages to the world [50].

4.5 Strategic Implications of Using Botnets in Modern Conflicts

Botnets in general are technically less sophisticated than many other cyber attack methods, but they can still serve the purpose of disrupting normal online services and get high visibility by media. If this will be the aim of attackers, using botnets is an efficient addition to the political campaign or as an additional element in strategic conflict. Since botnets are difficult to dismantle in real-time and hard to investigate afterwards, one can use them as anonymous mercenaries for the political course. This tool is also very cheap compared to many other methods. Botnets for hire represents a flexible resource for political and criminal purposes. Pay as you go system offered by criminal markets will work as far as there is a territory that hosts or facilitates the botnet coordination.

The likely actors using botnets in the future conflicts will be cyber criminals for hire, rogue cyber proxies, terrorists and nation-states. Proxy actors will be most likely to be used to command botnets in future conflicts. As they are usually seasoned criminals with significant resources, they are not caught by law enforcement easily, and sometimes could enjoy the protection by certain governments.

Botnets are cheap methods that allow to gain strategic advantages with little resources. This is the major reason for their use in future conflicts and for rapidly growing cyber espionage race too. Espionage with cyber tools is especially smooth as there is no use for infiltration, no risky human intelligence blunders etc.

The ultimate consequence of using cyber methods in conflicts and in espionage might contribute to the changing nature of conflicts themselves. Because of the world getting used to cyber tools, we might see the changes how power differentials will be perceived in conflicts and how conflicts will be carried out. Cyber tools will be used to facilitate the political aims in the conflicts, and therefore, they could be used for a number of different purposes. They could include hacking the military weapon systems to gain strategic advantages, sabotaging functioning of critical infrastructures, cutting off the ability to communicate, disrupting the possibility of strategic decision-making in international organisation, organising a highly visible DDOS to coerce a political challenger etc. Because of availability of cyber methods, conflicts can change too. As we have seen only the early years of conflicts with cyber elements used, and mainly increasing cyber espionage, it will be hard to predict how cyber methods will change the nature or conflicts or the way how people perceive the conflicts. One possibility will be that physical destruction will not be an aim in the future conflicts. In increasingly network-dependent societies in the future it might be enough to create a perception of a conflict with the disruption of Internet. How to gain the same psychological effect with cyber tools as was gained with air raids in the WW II, remains to be seen.

A danger might be that destructive cyber tools will be used in conflicts before there are rules in place how these tools should be used. Therefore, governments need urgently act to agree on a set of rules and norms that will guide the behavior of nation states in cyberspace.

5 National Policies and Organisational Measures to Address Cyber Threats

One of the central realisations in analysing different cyber threats, be them criminal or national security related, is the fact that the stress should be on general prevention. Law enforcement needs to prevent cybercrime, and governments need to raise the resilience of critical national cyber assets in order to raise the costs for attackers and protect security interests of the country. In the end, most preventive measures will be very similar and there are common requirements, guidelines and practices that all nations follow when building national cyber systems.

This chapter will discuss the policies and organisational countermeasures that are needed for successful fight with cyber threats at national level, including botnet mitigation. It will offer recommendations how to structure national cyber system and will also touch upon law enforcement requirements, and Internet Service Providers' responsibilities in fighting cyber threats.

5.1 Strategic Vision and a Balanced Regulatory Approach for National Cyber Resilience

As all countries depend on Information and Communication Technology they should adopt a model how to obtain a sufficient level of national cyber resilience. There are different models how exactly to achieve this goal, but the basic elements are the same in each country.

First important element is to introduce a strategic vision and relevant policies for cyber security. It could be done by developing a national cyber security strategy or a similar policy document. Achieving national vision in cyber security should naturally involve aspects of technology, but it should also involve a complex system of social interactions and processes that are much more crucial than technology. Processes and organisational mechanisms—coordination and cooperation, are hard to overestimate in cyber security of any organisation, and are absolutely a key at the national level.

Secondly, achieving the state of national cyber security is a process that never ends and it will require competence, and coordination efforts to win this uphill struggle. In order to achieve better security the traditional boundaries between the private and public, internal and external, civilian and military should be crossed on daily basis. Since these boundaries do not apply to cyber threats, they do not apply to cyber response either. In order to respond effectively, only the system that recognises the fundamental issue of blurred boundaries, will be successful. This is especially difficult to achieve in hierarchical organisations and countries, where institutional silos often pre-determine the way how policy response to cyber threats will be tailored. A successful operational policy response should include certain elements of networks and informal cooperation.

Each society will benefit from raising competence in cyber security in the whole society, from prioritizing education and training, and from investments in people. It is equally important to organise cyber security at national level. It would be ideal to have one institution that will take the lead in national cyber effort and facilitate coordination efforts between different national agencies and ministries. At the strategic level, the National Cyber Security Council should be created to take the most important decisions, while a parallel working level policy-making body from different agencies and ministries would coordinate and solve routine issues.

5.1.1 Layers of National Cyber Security Coordination

The first, and the most fundamental layer is the coordination between the technical experts who are responsible for mitigating IT risks in private and public organisations that provide critical services for the country. The technical experts are often the "first line of national cyber defence", and therefore, their expertise and skills in recognising the attack patterns, mitigating and passing information on to other IT experts constitute an invaluable part of national cyber efforts.

The other layers of national cyber coordination are related to organisational coordination issues, national policy processes and strategic decision-making. Because of many intertwined dimensions in cyber incidents and cyber threats, there should be a sufficient number of policymakers in key organisations of law enforcement, national security, defence and internal security who can understand the threats in cyberspace and how cyber threats can cause effects in physical world. The existence of "cyber educated" policy generalists is a very important layer for national cyber policy coordination, because this community should assess the political impact of technical incidents, should recognise new policy require-ments stemming from a changed threat situation, and should be regularly inform-ing the top-level decision-makers on the situation in cyber front.

The working level experts coordination consists of mid-level managers in differ-ent organisations who are responsible for cyber security policy related tasks in their respective organisations. This group does not have to have technical background, but could be a network of public servants in national security or internal security policy-making community educated as lawyers, political scientists etc. In the private sector, the same layer would correspond to the company risk managers and IT risk managers.

The third coordination layer that is decisive, be it at the national level or in any organisation, is the top level decision-makers that should tackle cyber issues as one among many other critical issues. They should learn to see cyber threats as a new dimension in overall risk management. At the national level that top layer for cyber security decision-making should be determined wisely. They need to be decision-makers who are above the micromanagement level and in charge of strategic decisions of their respective agencies or government departments. They should have enough authority to decide for a ministry or a company in the field of cyber security. They should not be the Heads of IT Departments, or CISOs, but general managers a level or two higher in order to see wider horizon and have authority over strategic decision-making in their organisations' activities and budget allocations. They are key persons since they will have a responsibility to place cyber issues in the strategic context of national security. The last require-ment is that most senior national cyber security decision-making body should have a direct link to national security decision-making. For instance, the National Cyber Security Council should report directly to the National Security Council.

5.1.2 Critical Information Infrastructure Protection and National Security

Updated technological and organisational security measures should be applied to strengthen national cyber resilience. The key issue to be solved is how to define these IT systems where extra security measures should be applied. The common advice is to first concentrate on the most critical systems where dedicate serious national cyber security resources, and secondly, make sure there is enough public awareness in society that also non-critical computer system owners will protect their information systems properly. The principle of cyber security as a shared responsibility of all citizens and organisations in society should be stressed in national cyber strategy.

5.1.3 Public–Private Partnership and Proportional Regulation

Once the nation knows what are the most critical services, it would be useful to map critical IT services that support the critical services. For this process, a public–private and private–private partnerships could be created with a central governmental agency offering incentives to different players in the stakeholder group. Governments need to show initiative in launching this kind of partnership and raise awareness on cyber issues in private sector companies. Governments could offer a few incentives, like coordination, training or better overview on dependencies between different private sector services. Majority of private sector principals would welcome if governments will take a role of a coordinator and awareness raiser in national cyber security.

Countries should aid light regulation for critical service providers, where cyber issues are seen in the context of critical services and national security. Cyber component should be mainstreamed into general risk management and should be included to overall reporting requirement as well as into country's crisis management system.

Overregulating could be worse than not regulating at all. Regulation should provide a light regulatory framework with cyber-specific requirements for critical service providers, such as compulsory IT audits, an obligation to notify if service cannot be provided for certain time period, and an obligation to report on serious incidents and disruptions to the sectoral authority. IT security risks should be part of general risk management of critical service providers.

The approach that seems to work, is to take a sectoral approach to critical service providers. The authority to oversee the private sector service providers should be delegated to the sectoral regulator. The sectoral regulators have to deal also with mandating IT risk assessments in their respective sectors, and if not already there, to add IT risks to the regulatory framework. This will guarantee placing the responsibility for cyber security where it belongs. Sectoral approach should be accompanied with an effective national coordination mechanism. National cyber authority will conduct oversight and provide assistance in IT specific risk management issues.

Countries should also have an efficient judicial system and legal framework in place to facilitate cybercrime investigations and prosecution, which will be discussed below in more detail.

5.1.4 Education, Training and Awareness

A very important component in a national cyber effort is raising awareness on cyber threats among larger public and educating the IT workforce. Cyber security is very similar to secure traffic where certain security culture is needed. Creating cyber security culture can be accomplished only by raising awareness of all computer users and investing to people's e-skills. In this respect, all individuals have a great role to play in creating a more secure information society in the long run.

In addition to educating the public, the state should guarantee that IT workforce has high level of competence in information security. Updating practical skills of IT security specialists and providing graduate education are the key factors. The human factor is going to be a strategic element in building a more secure information society in the future. Advancing skills of IT specialists will also provide for more efficient incident response and mitigation technics in cyber crises.

5.2 National and International Requirements for Investigation of Cybercrime

In essence, fighting with cybercrime is similar to fighting with any other crime. It just requires more of special know-how. Cybercriminals need to launder money and they use people to cash money. This process leaves traces for operational police forces.

The difficulty with fighting cybercrime lies in the fact that organised crime occurs in many jurisdictions simultaneously, and criminals change their locations swiftly. Therefore, any successful investigation should be supported by many pre-existing factors, e.g. existence of cybercrime legislation, judicial support in each jurisdiction, cooperation networks with private sector and Internet Service Providers, international police cooperation, information sharing, adequate crime reporting etc. In order to fight cybercrime effectively, all these elements need to be in place beforehand. Each country should have specialised units for cybercrime and regional units. The existence of these units facilitates 24/7 police cooperation and international investigations.

A keyword in addressing cybercrime is prevention. Prevention includes timely reporting, information sharing, training and raising competence. Cybercrime reporting will be essential for realistic assessment of threats. Reporting is sometimes difficult because not all companies would like to disclose their losses, and the scope of breaches in their systems. Inadequate crime reporting is one of the major hurdles in assessing the severity and scope of botnets.

As in any other professional community, the police community fighting cybercrime will benefit from best professional practices' exchange. Sharing best practices, collecting and analysing information are key factors here. Information and intelligence sharing will be successful if done in close cooperation with private sector, and CERT community.

Fighting cybercrime needs specialised training on how to collect electronic evidences, and how to arrest criminals so that they will not have a chance to delete or destroy materials etc. A very important part of cybercrime prevention is forensics training—Internet forensics and reverse engineering capabilities are major building blocks in cyber security capacity.

A major difficulty in international investigations is presented by different legal procedures and penalties for cybercrime across countries. Harmonising legal frameworks that allow criminalise computer crime is becoming a key public policy issue that most countries work on. The only international instrument offering a model for minimum national standards in cybercrime legislation and requirements for international cooperation, the Budapest Convention or Council of Europe Convention for Cybercrime, is currently in adoption process in many countries outside Europe [51]. With promotion of Budapest Convention and with raising law enforcement capabilities, rapid spread of botnets and cybercrime could be curtailed.

5.3 Focus on Internet Service Providers

In addition to the efforts by governmental authorities, private sector plays a pivotal role in offering a secure cyber infrastructure. Private sector owns and manages practically all networks where end-users' data travel, and they also see the problems in the networks first.

The companies running the Internet infrastructure, the Internet Service providers, hosting companies, network providers and webmail providers constitute a major infrastructure where botnets are residing. Differences between these companies are huge depending on market share, size, and other factors. Research suggests that actually there is no evidence of smaller and less capitalised companies hosting more malicious activities, but large top 50 ISPs were found of connecting a half of compromised computers worlwide [52]. Although smaller ISPs are usually responsible for distributing spam it was revealed that external conditions did not affect security practices of ISP-s, but rather it was related to computer security awareness and procedures inside the specific company. However, few factors will facilitate ISP-s hosting botnets, such as using pirate software, and having no public policy by governments on cyber security. Similarly, the factors reducing the number of botnets in the networks is general level of education and technical competence in a country and the existence of governmental cyber security programmes [52].

As the large number of ISPs and network operators responsible for removing botnet infrastructure are major players, the efforts of governments in suggesting different regulatory approaches should be easier. Cyber experts Melissa Hathaway and John Savage suggest that similarly to other sectors, government requirements should raise the general security standard also in telecommunications sector. They offer eight duties for the ISPs that could be either mandated by law or expected by governments under public–private partnership arrangements [53].

The first duty is to provide a reliable and accessible conditions for Internet traffic and services. Currently, ISPs inform customers of botnets on voluntary basis, but there is no uniform standard of operating for all companies worldwide. Since this is a global industry, governments could issue a collection of good practices that ISPs should follow for staying or entering into Internet connection business. Internet is an increasingly critical backbone infrastructure for the digital economy and will contribute to economic growth, therefore, the current model of regulating this market should be rethought.

The second duty will be to provide authentic routing information, and make sure that more secure Border Gateway Protocols (BGP) are used in routing business worldwide. This duty stems from the fact that BGPs' vulnerabilities can be easily exploited by criminal groups or proxy actors, and using more secure protocols is needed for a more reliable underlying Internet infrastructure.

The third duty is to provide authentic naming information in the Domain Name System (DNS). In order to avoid misuing the current DNS system, a more secure DNSSEC system should become prevalent in everyday management of DNS architecture, including by the ISPs.

The fourth duty requires that anonymised security incident statistics should be revealed to the public. One of the major issues in finding a proper public policy response to botnets relates to the lack of reliable incident data, and the resistance of companies to reveal the real magnitude of security incidents. If the ISPs would collectively participate in creating an anonymous clearinghouse of security incidents statistics, the quality of reporting the data could improve.

The fifth duty includes educating the customers about security threats. As ISPs see the threats most clearly in real-time, it would be logical to assume that they also conduct early warning on threats to all stakeholders they depend on. This will require additional efforts to reach out to different groups of customers and ISPs can reach these different groups more easily than any other institution in Internet economy. Few successful private-private and public–private educational campaigns exist that could provide a model [53].

The sixth duty demands that ISPs should notify their customers on infections in their infrastructures. Sophistication and frequency of cybercrime incidents clearly calls for a right response by those running this infrastructure. Web-based attacks, and botnets in mobile devices are shaking user confidence in Internet economy. The best practices in informing customers deployed in Australia, Japan, Finland, Germany and many countries already could be extended worldwide.

The seventh duty consists of an ISP warning requirement on imminent threat and assistance in emergency situation. ISPs have an overview on malware in their networks and have also to provide uninterrupted services. They can block the infected computers used in DDOS attacks, and can warn other players. They have showed the ability to act swiftly during the most notorius DDOS attacks against Estonia, Georgia, the US, and Palestine. A responsibility to collectively defend the common Internet infrastructure by early warning and helping in cyber emergencies could be inserted to the best ISP practices worldwide.

The eight duty is to avoid aiding and abetting criminal activity in networks. ISPs have a global reach and could be exploited for criminal activity. They have a duty to aid law enforcement, and avoid assisting, even indirectly, any form of illegal activity present in their networks [54].

Additionally, initiating global cooperation between the companies that operate the networks and provide Internet services should be considered as an option [55].

5.4 Examples of Existing Anti-Botnet Initiatives

There are a few global initiatives to share best practices and raise awareness on the botnets. FIRST, the global organisation for Computer Incident Response Teams, has launched a Botnet Mitigation and Remediation Special Interest Group. This initiative aims at studying different initiatives around the world that detect and mitigate botnet and malware infections. For example, organizations that provide data feeds and CSIRTs that are helping to set up national cleaning centers. FIRST botnet group aims at assessing the effectiveness of these initiatives and collecting data on the best mitigation models. Although many existing collaboration initiatives are in place, there are so far very few countries were the level of infection is relatively low.

Most cybersecurity incidents should be mitigated at the national level. Therefore the national initiatives for cleaning networks from botnets should be encouraged and good models should be circulated how to do this successfully.

In the Netherlands, the biggest ISPs with 90 % of market share have formed a voluntary network called Anti-Botnet Working Group. The aim is to inform customers if their machines were infected, and if needed, also to quarantine some machines. However, the effectiveness of these measures should be studied further. A recent study ordered by the Dutch Ministry of Foreign Affairs shows that the number of infected machines in the Netherlands was ca 10 % in 2010, which was OECD average [56]. Most infections occurred in the three largest ISP networks. The ISPs contact customers with only most serious infections, and the practices of different ISP vary greatly.

The Japanese Cyber Clean Center represents a more institutionalised approach towards fighting botnets. The Center aims at preventing, helping and cleaning users' computers from malware, with cooperation of ISPs [57]. The center acts also as a coordination platform between ISPs, technology companies providing solutions and end-users.

Germany has an Anti Botnet Advisory Center, financed by the Ministry of Interior and supported by the BSI (Federal Office for Information Security) and ISPs. It provides free software for computer scan and a practical three-step guidance to disinfect the computer by the end-user. It also lists hotlines of the ISPs [58]. This customer friendly approach seems to appeal to an average user who needs advice on computers.

However, with many other good initiatives in place most studies point that the prospect of infections at the national level is increasing, specially in the countries with high-speed Internet [59].

The most effective botnet mitigation cases have been private sector led take-down activities targeting specific criminal botnets, such as Conficker, Mariposa or

Bredolab. These have been carried out intensively during a short period by a significant number of interested stakeholders and had then slowed down once their goals had been achieved.

Therefore, further studies would be welcome that bring together experts and identify success factors in botnet mitigation and remediation, and best practices. As the countries in the most infected list tend to be the same, there might be an added value of an independent study that measures effectiveness of botnet mitigation initiatives.

6 International Cooperation and Capacity Building as Cornerstone for Better Global Cybersecurity

Cyber threats are fast evolving and do not recognise borders. Each cyber incident involves multiple jurisdictions and it is extremely difficult for law enforcement and other governmental authorities to address this new threat without extensive international cooperation. Mitigation of botnets, and addressing cybercrime offenses in general is difficult to investigate and prosecute. Many technologically less advanced countries in the world are not able to tackle cybercrime on their territory, and might offer safe havens for cyber criminals or for cyber proxies. Against this background, the international organised cybercrime networks have grown ever more powerful, increasing so the vulnerabilities for advanced industrial economies. The networks run by criminals could be also rented by hostile nation states or terrorists.

As cybercriminal networks are transnational and global, so requires the cybercrime investigation broad international judiciary and law enforcement cooperation. Currently, the capacity of law enforcement to deal with cybercriminal organisations poses a global challenge. It is difficult to reach out to the regions in the world where cyber security capacity in many countries is limited and legal frameworks are missing. In order to carry out successful international cybercrime investigations, the international organisations and advanced economies should intensify cooperation, as well as cyber security capacity building efforts in emerging markets and developing countries.

A central issue in international cooperation is the existence of legal framework that allows investigation and prosecution of cybercrime, as well as capacity to address cyber threats with technological and organisational measures. The following chapter will describe the international initiatives contributing to European cyber security and will offer recommendations for capacity building efforts in emerging and developing countries.

6.1 The Overview of International Initiatives to Address Cyber Threats and Cybercrime

There are already significant efforts undertaken by several international organisations and countries to take systemic measures in order to kick off policies to counter cyber threats. Many actors concentrate on enhancing international coop-eration and supporting cyber security capacity building. The Council of Europe has been promoting the Council of Europe Convention on Cybercrime and train-ing judiciary and law enforcement personnel. The Council of Europe Global Cybercrime Project has already reached more than 100 countries in promoting the CoE Convention of Cybercrime. The EU, EU member states, many international organisations, and other industrialised countries have engaged in law enforcement training and cyber security capacity building in the developing countries. The U.S. government and academia have been involved in various capacity building efforts since the dawn of Internet.

6.1.1 The Council of Europe

The cornerstone of successful law enforcement cooperation in addressing cyber-crime is the legal framework that supports timely operational activities, investi-gation and prosecution of criminal actors exploiting cyberspace. The Council of Europe has launched a number of initiatives in training experts and develop-ing national legislation according to the principles of the Council of Europe Convention on Cybercrime.

The Council of Europe Convention on Cybercrime (Budapest Convention) represents a central international law instrument that lays legal standards for countries to aid investigation of cybercrime. The Convention also facilitates inter-national cooperation in investigating cyber incidents, and serves as a model law worldwide. In addition to promoting the Convention, Council of Europe has been training law enforcement and judicial authorities, issued guidelines for national cyber security, for public–private cooperation and for international cooperation.

Council of Europe Global Project on Cybercrime has supported since its launch in 2006 several hundred activities in some 120 countries worldwide. These include harmonisation of legislation, law enforcement and judicial training, pub-lic–private cooperation and international cooperation. The project is funded by Estonia, Japan, Monaco, Romania, Microsoft, McAfee and Visa Europe as well as from the budget of the Council of Europe [60]. Annual Octopus conferences on cooperation against cybercrime have been organised with a large number of key international participants.

Within the global project, several useful regional and national programmes are funded. Project on Cybercrime in Georgia assisted Georgia in adoption of legisla-tion on cybercrime and on the protection of personal data, design of a high-tech crime unit and of training programmes for judges and prosecutors [61].

EU and CoE joint project on cooperation against cybercrime in EU pre-acces-sion countries in 2010–2013 covers eight countries and areas in South-Eastern Europe. Launched in November 2010, it focuses on cybercrime policies and strat-egies, harmonisation of legislation, international cooperation, law enforcement training, financial investigations, law enforcement and service providers coopera-tion [62].

Another joint EU and CoE Eastern Partnership regional project on Cybercrime was launched in April 2011 in six countries of Eastern Europe 2011–2013. It provides advice and assesses measures taken with regard to cybercrime legislation, specialised institutions, judicial and law enforcement training, financial investigations, and international cooperation [63].

6.1.2 The European Union

In order to successfully address cyber threats, including the criminal botnet infrastructure, it is extremely important that the EU has a common legal approach to cybercrime. The EU has made several attempts towards this common approach since 2005.

In 2005, a Council Framework Decision on Attacks on Information Systems (2005/222/JHA) was adopted, which seeks to approximate criminal law across the EU to ensure that Europe's law enforcement and judicial authorities can take action against this form of crime. The decision recognised the disparities in member states in criminal law and the need for effective police cooperation within the Union. It also called for an information exchange mechanism between the member states [64].

In 2007, the Commission communication "Towards a general policy on the fight against cyber crime" was issued that seeks to improve operational law enforcement cooperation, political cooperation and coordination between Member States, political and legal cooperation with third countries as well as awareness raising, training, research and a reinforced dialogue with industry and possible legislative action.

In October 2010 a new EU Internal Security Strategy was adopted that elevates cyber security to a key concern for the EU. The strategy aims at raising levels of security for citizens and businesses in cyberspace and tackle the cybercrime at a qualitative level. Three specific proposals in the strategy include the establishment of an EU cybercrime centre by the 2013, the establishment of a network of Computer Emergency Response Teams in all EU institutions by 2012 and launching of a European information sharing and alert system, EISAS, by 2013 [65].

Additionally, in 2010, a proposal was developed to adopt a relevant directive for member states in advancing their capabilities in fighting with cyber crime. The need for the new directive was based on a Commission review on the implementation of the Framework Directive on Information System Attacks. The analysis concluded that additional work needs to be done to harmonise the legal framework within the EU for the fight with cybercrime, specially in the background of new sophisticated attack methods and technologies [66].

In addition to plans to significantly improve cybercrime legislation, the EU has also a well-functioning network of national cybercrime units. The heads of national units meet regularly under the formal heading of the EU High Tech Crime Units taskforce. The EU taskforce works closely with the Europol and Interpol high tech crime departments, and links also up with its U.S. and other international counterparts. In order to aid cyber crime investigation and information exchange between member states, the EU Cybercrime Center was established in 2013 [67].

Botnet mitigation is directly related to the regulatory framework in the EU telecommunications sector. The EU Telecommunications Framework Directive, or the collection of amendments of former directives (2009/140/EC) was adopted in 2009 that issues also new security regulations for the telecommunications sector. Provision 13 A introduces the mandatory incident reporting for the Internet Security Providers, demands the member states to apply appropriate risk management measures to ensure the level of telecommunications services. If adviced by ENISA, the Commission may mandate the member states to adopt the technical measures based on international standards for communication networks security [68].

The European Commission Directorate General for Information Society has prepared the EU Critical Information Infrastructure Protection policy "Protecting Europe from large scale cyber-attacks and disruptions: enhancing preparedness, security and resilience".[5] The policy was endorsed at the EU ministerial meeting in Tallinn in April 2009, and aims at creating EU-wide coordination, prevention and response mechanisms for cyber incidents. As a part of this process, the regular pan-European cyber exercises have started in 2010 with support of the European Network and Information Security Agency (ENISA) [69].

6.1.3 Other International Cooperation Initiatives

G-8 24/7 network for cybercrime represents a global list of contact points within the law enforcement authorities. It aids rapid operational cooperation in investigating and prosecuting high tech crimes.

In addition to formal initiatives, few very well-established informal forums exist in cyber security field that provide for policy development and exchange of best practices. The Meridian process handles the only regularly updated global reference book for Critical Information Infrastructure Protection policies and points of contacts for technical cyber emergencies in more than 50 countries. As this forum is limited to governmental representatives only, it connects cyber security policy and technical experts. Meridian has annual and regional events, and serves as a major global trust-building and consultation forum in cyber security policies. The Meridian network also issues recommendations, shares best practices, offers IT security standard setting guidelines, and other information for its participants.

FIRST connects the CERT-s all over the world, and serves as a forum for technical community. At FIRST conferences IT security specialists exchange information and experiences in incident handling practices, and build the personal

---

[5] Communication from the Commission to the European Parliament, the Council, the European Economic and Social Committee and the Committee of the Regions on Critical Information Infrastructure Protection—Protecting Europe from large scale cyber-attacks and disruptions: enhancing preparedness, security and resilience {SEC(2009) 399} {SEC(2009) 400}, COM/2009/0149 final.

contacts that will be very useful in times of cyber crises. There are plenty of information security expert forums, which serve the same purposes, and have been so far the major mechanisms in connecting the professionals whose everyday work is to guarantee stability of the global ICT sector. In the absence of institutional crises management mechanisms, these informal networks have saved the Internet many times.

6.2 International Capacity Building to Address Cyber Threats and Cybercrime

Capacity-building in cyber security is one of the policy areas that has been articulated as a priority for achieving a more reliable global cyberspace. At the London Conference for Cyberspace in 2011, one of the major conclusions was that cyber security is a global concern and all countries need to be closely involved in countering cyber threats [70].

However, not all the countries in the world have equal technical capabilities, preparedness and legal framework to address cyber threats. Many policy-makers nowadays are looking for models of how to structure the capacity building efforts, what methods to use and how to measure the efficiency of these efforts. There are few key issues in capacity building that should be brought into attention of policy-makers.

First, capacity building in cyber security should be coupled with efforts of building safer and more reliable connections and communication networks worldwide. The aim should be to add the security elements already into the package while extending the communication networks into new markets, choosing an IT architecture and developing software. As this aim requires also more attention to security features by major private sector players, public–private partnership is required to build a more reliable and secure global cyber infrastructure.

The second important element in cyber security capacity building is to keep in mind that cyber security in one nation will depend on the awareness and cooperation of many players in other nations. In order to tackle cyber threats efficiently, the law enforcement agencies should closely link up with CERTs, Internet Service Providers and public–private partnership networks. Equally important is to have a proper legal framework in place for facilitating investigation and timely prosecution of cyber offences. The key issue is to invest into training and education, including broad base of e-skills of the public, computer security knowledge among law enforcement, IT professionals and other relevant national stakeholders.

The third element is to facilitate international and regional cooperation in each field of cyber security: law enforcement, critical infrastructure protection, CERT networks, and national security communities. Better cyber security will be always a result of coordination and cooperation among a wide range of players.

To contribute to this new policy field, the recommendations for capacity building in cybercrime and incident response will be outlined below.

6.2.1 Key Capabilities in Addressing Cybercrime

At national strategic and policy-making level the countries should have a policy towards addressing cybercrime that will create a comprehensive national approach, and help to engage important decision-makers. Ideally, efforts fighting cybercrime should be seen as a part of a broader national strategy in cyber security, which should bring together different stakeholders and facilitate cooperation between different national agencies.

An important part of national cyber efforts is to ensure that a country has updated cybercrime legislation in place. This includes measures to criminalise offences related to computer crime, and harmonise the minimum penalties with general international practice. It will be also important to guarantee that procedural law tools for efficient investigations exist. It would be ideal to follow a model of Budapest Convention on Cybercrime to make sure that necessary safeguards and conditions exist for investigation process.

At operational level it will be crucial to have an adequate overview on the situation to understand the threats, trends and patterns of cybercrime. It would be equally important to establish a reporting mechanism of cybercrime incidents for individuals and for public and private sector organisations.

In order to assist law enforcement investigations, the police forces need to have special cybercrime or high-tech crime units with dedicated computer crime experts. The experts should master a certain level of knowledge on how to collect evidence and should be supported by computer forensic experts.

The operational police units should be supported by the similar units within judiciary authorities for efficient prosecution.

Education, training and awareness are the fields where significant attention should be devoted. For better cyber security culture in a country there is a need for awareness of general public of computer users and society in general on cyber threats. Awareness should also reach mid and top management of public and private sector decision-makers to facilitate the protection of critical information systems.

It will be equally important to concentrate on law enforcement and judicial training. This will include skills to investigate cybercrime, e.g. secure electronic evidence, focus on forensic analyses, and competence on network security. Specific skills should be obtained by experts at different levels of investigation and prosecution process. For latter, initial, in-service and advanced training for judges and prosecutors on cybercrime and electronic evidence should be conducted. Judges and prosecutors specialising on cybercrime cases should also have a minimal understanding on technical issues.

Law enforcement can effectively operate only in close contact with relevant stakeholders in private sector. Public–private cooperation in cybercrime reporting systems, information and intelligence sharing is essential.

6.2.2 Capacity Building in Incident Management in Developing Countries

Many developing countries have very limited capacity to monitor and manage the incidents in cyberspace. To build this capacity, they need to introduce technological and organisational measures for better incident management. The minimum requirements are needed for setting up the national Computer Emergency Response Teams (CERTs), including specialised training, acquiring equipment and exchange of best practices within the international professional CERT networks.

Effective cyber security capacity building needs a functioning national CERT, which will be the center of the coordination efforts in a country and feeds information to law enforcement and acts as an interface between the government agencies and private sector. CERT, private sector and information security networks in a country need to be brought together for long-term sustainable incident response and monitoring system.

Experience has shown the positive effects of peer pressure in cyber security awareness building happens on regional basis, which helps to maintain the sustainable developments after initial assistance programs have ended. The regional model works if to start with more advanced countries in a specific region, and form a group of leading countries that will later continue to drive cyber security efforts in the region.

Cyber security activities need to take into account the networked nature of this domain and include all stakeholders. The number of stakeholders in cyber security is high and capacity building approach must be coherent across borders and consistent over time. Attention should be on prevention and it is crucial to invest in cross-border prevention strategies and mechanisms highlighting the importance of everybody's involvement. Actors must understand their roles and adopt a scalable and flexible approach, they should strengthen public–private cooperation as well as private sector responses. It will be important to coordinate and de-conflict various funding initiatives already underway.

Successful capacity building will promote a community building approach and cooperation frameworks. Stakeholders need to be engaged in a positive environment and in a community-based environment built on the principle of reciprocity. Approach must be coherent across borders, consistent over time, scalable and flexible. Donors should be building on existing efforts, coordinating and de-conflicting where necessary. National counterparts must take clear ownership of any new capability and must make sure the efforts will be sustainable in long run.

CERTs should be the primary focus of capacity building because they facilitate the overall national coordination process. Encouraging voluntary and informal cooperation will bring value for all those involved. Personal motivation of informal networks will be important for the private sector, which needs incentives and can so build on successes. In incidence response, the principle of reciprocity is crucial. CERTs build trust-based networks on all continents with many actors recognizing that the nature of a national incident response relies heavily on international cooperation.

Capacity building will be sustainable if there is public–private partnership, minimum national organisational and technological capacity in incident response and relevant institutional frameworks. The grassroots approach that harnesses local involvement and expertise has proven to be the most desirable approach to capacity building, but sometimes the clear commitment of national governments is required to guarantee high level political buy-in.

6.3 Conclusion

Botnets represent a fast developing global cyber security issue, facilitated by the low awareness of end-users, by huge differences in national legal and policy approaches to cyber security and by the lack of attention to security practices in companies providing Internet services. Botnets are used for reaping economic gains by cybercrime actors as well as for espionage and for other politically motivated activities. Although many efforts have been made recently in mitigating botnets, they will be likely to re-emerge at the new level of sophistication and organisation. Also, botnet activity will move away from developed countries and spread further in emerging markets and in developing countries.

In order to efficiently fight botnets, countries need to step up their efforts in building resilient national cyber security systems. National cyber resilience includes a sufficient legal framework to deal with cybercrime, advanced Critical Information Infrastructure Protection system, public–private partnership, education and training, national cyber security vision, policy and operational coordination mechanisms and a right approach to regulation. It will be also important that private sector will pay more attention to security issues. A new regulatory approach to Internet Service Providers will help to avoid even more contaminated networks in the future.

Serious cyber security incidents and crises need international response mechanisms, which should be advanced by intensified international cooperation and capacity building. A central concern in creating a more global approach towards addressing cyber threats is how to create minimum standards of preparedness of countries to deal with cyber incidents and cyber crime. In international context, it is especially important to ensure that all countries in the world have a national legal system that allows investigation and prosecution of cybercrime. They should also have a minimum capacity of law enforcement to address cyber crime. A third key issue is the technical preparedness for incident response. Without these three components in place in majority of countries worldwide, international cooperation on addressing cyber threats will be very difficult. Private sector should also play a role in global capacity building efforts.

Additionally, governments are not often in agreement on the future vision of cyberspace. Some of them would like to have a more controlled cyberspace using security as a pretext, and would like to justify state control over free flow of information and freedom of expression. In order to overcome the dilemma between freedom and security in cyberspace, the norms for responsible state behavior should be introduced. International community should seek for the ways to create more transparency and predictability in state activities, and apply international measures to enforce responsible behavior in cyberspace by nation states.

Further research on botnets will be desirable. Technical aspects of botnets will be developing fast because of considerable profits involved in cybercrime activity. In addition to research on how to detect, prevent and mitigate botnets, further studies are needed to assess economic loss caused by botnets in different economic sectors. In addition, more studies are needed that touch upon specific organisational and policy aspects in fighting different types of botnets. These should include detailed analyses on recent regional trends of botnet activity. A better overview on botnets will help the policy-makers to allocate resources for capacity building, and to tailor necessary regulatory requirements that all ISPs should follow in order to address this global issue.

References

1. Rowinski, D. (2011). Cybecrime as large as illegal drug trade. *Symantec Reports*. Retrieved September 8, 2011, from http://www.readwriteweb.com/archives/symantec_cybercrime_as_large_as_the_illegal_drug_t.php.
2. Europol presentation at the: Round table on cyber security: Which role for the European Parliament? *European Parliament Workshop of Cybercrime*. November 22, 2011.
3. Hogben, G., Plohmann, D., Gerhards-Padilla, E., Leder, F. (2012). Botnets: Detection, measurement, disinfection and defence. *ENISA Report*, March 7, 2012.
4. Lewis, J. A. (2012). Significant cyber incidents since 2006. *Publication of the Center for Strategic and International Studies*, May 4, 2012.
5. Hogben, G., Plohmann, D., Gerhards-Padilla, E., Leder, F. (2011). Botnets: Ten tough questions, *ENISA Report*, 2011.
6. Microsoft Security Intelligence Report, January–June 2009.
7. Hogben, G., Plohmann, D., Gerhards-Padilla, E., Leder, F. (2012). Botnets: Detection, measurement, disinfection and defence. *ENISA Report*, March 7, 2012.
8. van Eeten, M. et al. (2010). *The role of internet service providers in botnet mitigation: An empirical analysis based on spam data. OECD Science, Technology and Industry Working Papers*, 2010/05, OECD Publishing.
9. Armin, J. et al. (2012) Top 50 bad hosts and networks. *HostExploit's Worldwide Cybercrime Series 1st Quarter Report*, April 2012.
10. Gross, G. (2012). Cybersecurity bill would create costly regulations, say critics. *ITNews*, February 16, 2012.
11. Africa used as botnet army; South East Asia invests in information warfare; Latin America beefs up regulation, *Info-Security Magazine*, July 30, 2012.
12. Empsak, J. (2012). How banking trojans empty your online accounts. *NBCNews*, April 24, 2012.
13. White house announces public-private partnership initiative to combat botnets. *Press Release*, The U.S. Department of Commerce, May 30, 2012.
14. Kirk, J. (2012). Microsoft leads seizure of Zeus-related cybercrime servers. *NetworkWorld*, March 26, 2012.
15. Magnuson, S. (2010). Russian cyberthief case illustrates security risks for U.S. corporations. *National Defence Magazine*, May 2010.
16. Armin, J. (2011). The carbon market, cyber attacks and organised criminal gangs. *Hostexploit*, January 27, 2011.
17. Palo Alto networks discover "Jericho" an emerging botnet. *Spamfighter News*, May 12, 2012.
18. Krebs, B. (2008). Host of internet spam is cut off. *Washington Post*, November 12, 2008.

19. Leyden, J. (2011). Rustock takedown: How the world's worst botnet was KO'd. *The Register*, March 23, 2011.
20. Rustock. *Special Edition Security Intelligence Report: Battling the Rustock Threat*, March 16, 2011.
21. Schwartz, M. J. (2010). Bredolab botnet still spewing malware. *Information Week*, October 29, 2010.
22. Huge spam botnet Grum is taken out by security researchers. *BBC News*, July 19, 2012.
23. Ryan, J. (2012). DHS: Hackers mounting organised cyber attack on U.S. gas pipelines. *ABC News*, May 9, 2012.
24. In the dark: Crucial industries confront cyberattacks, *McAfee Report*, 2011.
25. Williams, C. (2011). GCHQ aims to protect critical private networks from hackers, *The Telegraph*, March 8, 2011.
26. Internet based attacks on critical systems rise, *BBC News*, April 18, 2011.
27. Clayton, M. (2011). FBI to kill secret-stealing Russian botnet: Is your computer infected? *The Christian Scince Monitor*, May 6, 2011.
28. How conficker continues to propagate. *Microsoft Security Intelligence Report*, vol. 12, 2011.
29. Willsher, K. (2009). French fighter planes grounded by computer virus. *The Telegraph*, February 7, 2009.
30. Researcher warns of Android phone "botnet". *Yahoo News*, July 5, 2012.
31. Georgia tech information security center and Georgia tech research Institute "Emerging Cyber Threats Report 2012", *Georgia Tech Cyber Security Summitt 2011*.
32. Brooks, C. (2011). Cybersecurity experts say small businesses beware, *Business News Daily*, October 9, 2011.
33. Demchak, C. (2012). Resilience, disruption, and a "Cyber Westphalia": Options for national security in a cybered conflict world. In N. Burns, J. Price (Eds.), *Securing cyberspace: A new domain for national security*. Queenstown: Aspen Institute.
34. Nathan, T. (2005). Inside the Chinese hack attack, *Time*, August 25, 2005.
35. Winkler, I. (2005). Guard against titan rain hackers, *Computer World*, October 20, 2005.
36. Clarke, R. A. (2012). How China steals our secrets. *New York Times*, April 2, 2012.
37. Deibert, R., Rohozinski, R. (2009). Tracking ghostnet: Investigating a cyber espionage network, *Information Warfare Monitor*, March 29, 2009.
38. Zetter, K. (2010). Google hack attack was ultra sophisticated, New details Show, *Wired*, January 14, 2010.
39. Alperovitch, D. (2011). Revealed: operation shady RAT, *McAfee White Paper*, Retrieved August 3, 2011 from http://www.mcafee.com/us/resources/white-papers/wp-operation-shady-rat.pdf.
40. Lewis, J. A. (2012). Significant cyber incidents since 2006, *Publication of the Center for Strategic and International Studies*, May 4, 2012.
41. Olsen, K. (2009). Massive cyber attack knocked out government web sites starting on July 4, *Huffington Post*, July 9, 2009.
42. Leyden, J. (2011). Palestine fingers Israel for blasting Gaza off the net: Services wiped out in DDOS attack, *The Register*, November 2, 2011.
43. Duma Delegation Visits Estonia, *Postimees*, May 02, 2007.
44. Estonia's decision to dismantle the monument to soviet soldier desecrates WWII history, *Pravda*, April 26, 2007.
45. Digital fear emerge after data siege in Estonia, *New York Times*, May 29, 2007.
46. The hackers take down the most wired country in Europe, *The Wired*, August 21, 2007.
47. Senators quizz government for cybersecurity initiative. *Security Focus*, May 5, 2008.
48. Danchev, D. (2008). Coordinated Russia vs Georgia cyber attack in progress. *Zdnet.com*, August 11, 2008.
49. Leidner, J. (2008). Bear prints found on Georgian cyber-attacks. *The Register*, August 14, 2008.
50. Krebs, B. (2008). Report: Russian hacker forums fueled Georgia cyber attacks. *The Washington Post*, October 16, 2008.

51. Council of Europe treaty office website. http://conventions.coe.int/Treaty/Commun/ChercheSig. asp?NT=185&CL=ENG.
52. van Eeten, M. et al. (2010). The role of internet service providers in botnet mitigation: An empirical analysis based on spam data, *OECD science, Technology and Industry Working Papers*, 2010/05, OECD Publishing.
53. Hathaway, M. E. & John E. S. (2012). Duties for internet service providers. *Paper*, Munk School of Global Affairs, University of Toronto, March 2012.
54. Hathaway, M. E. (2012). Falling prey to cybercrime: Implications for business and the economy. Chap. 6 in *Securing cyberspace: A new domain for national security*. Queenstown: Aspen Institute.
55. Hathaway, M. E. (2012). Internet service providers are the front line of cyber-defence, *Europe's World,* Spring 2012.
56. van Eeten, M. et al. (2011). Internet service providers and botnet mitigation: A fact-finding study on the Dutch market, Delft University of Technology, January 2011.
57. Cyber clean centre website. https://www.ccc.go.jp/en_index.html.
58. Website of the anti-botnet advisory center. https://www.botfrei.de/en/ueber.html.
59. Norton Cybercrime Report, Symantec 2012.
60. Global project on cybercrime (Phase 2), 1 March 2009–31 December 2011, *Council of Europe Final Project Report*, April 9, 2012.
61. Project on cybercrime in Georgia, Council of Europe website. http://www.coe.int/t/dghl/coop eration/economiccrime/cybercrime/cy_project_in_georgia/projectcyber_en.asp.
62. Cybercrime, council of Europe website. http://www.coe.int/t/DGHL/cooperation/economiccr ime/cybercrime/default_en.asp.
63. Cybercrime, council of Europe website. http://www.coe.int/t/DGHL/cooperation/economiccr ime/cybercrime/default_en.asp.
64. Council framework decision 2005/222/JHA of 24 February 2005 on attacks against information systems (pp. 0067–0071). *Official Journal of the European Union,* March 16, 2005.
65. The EU internal security strategy in action: Five steps towards a more secure Europe. COM(2010) 673 final, Brussels, November 22, 2010.
66. Commission to boost Europe's defences against cyber-attacks, *IP 12/1239*, Retrieved September 30, 2010, from http://europa.eu/rapid/pressReleasesAction.do?reference=IP/10/1239.
67. Communication from the commission to the European parliament, the council "Tackling crime in our digital age: Establishing a European cybercrime centre". *COM(2012) 140 final,* Brussels, March 28, 2012.
68. EU Directive 2009/136/EC of the European parliament and of the Council of 25 November 2009 amending Directives 2002/21/EC on a common regulatory framework for electronic communications networks and services, 2002/19/EC on access to, and interconnection of, electronic communications networks and associated facilities, and 2002/20/EC on the authorisation of electronic communications networks and services, *Official Journal of the European Union,* December 18, 2009.
69. Cyber   Europe   2012,   ENISA   website.   http://www.enisa.europa.eu/activities/ Resilience-and-CIIP/cyber-crisis-cooperation/cyber-europe/cyber-europe-2012.
70. London conference on cyberspace: Chair's statement. Retrieved November 2, 2012, from http://www.fco.gov.uk/en/news/latest-news/?view=PressS&id=685663282.

Botnets: How to Fight the Ever-Growing Threat on a Technical Level

Jan Gassen, Elmar Gerhards-Padilla and Peter Martini

Abstract Today's malware, short term for malicious software, poses one of the major threats to all currently operated computer systems. The scale of the problem becomes obvious by looking at the global economic loss caused by different kinds of malware, which is estimated to be more than US$10 billion every year. This particularly applies for botnets, which are a special kind of malware. In contrast to other kinds of malware, botnets utilize a hidden communication channel to receive commands from their operator and communicate their current status. The ability to execute almost arbitrary commands on the infected machines makes botnets a general-purpose tool to perform malicious cyber-activities. In this context, botnets are used for example by individual perpetrators, organized crime as well as governmentally supported organizations, in order to achieve individual gains. This chapter gives a technical insight into current botnet techniques and discusses state of the art countermeasures to combat the botnet threat in detail. This includes new detection methods as well as different approaches to actively compromise running botnets. Different techniques as well as their impact on current botnets are discussed, considering individual involved stakeholders. In addition to the technical countermeasures, current initiatives countering botnets are introduced.

1 Introduction

Today's computer systems face an unprecedented amount and versatility of cyber threats. Since the Internet was designed without explicitly considering security aspects, it has become the most frequently used medium for cyber criminals. It offers the opportunity of reaching billions of computer systems within milliseconds without the need of physical interference with the targeted system. Beyond that, it offers multiple possibilities to disguise the attacker's origin, which makes it difficult if not impossible to track down individual cyber criminals. It is therefore possible to launch large-scale cyber attacks without actually worrying about facing

H. Tiirmaa-Klaar et al., *Botnets*, SpringerBriefs in Cybersecurity,
DOI: 10.1007/978-1-4471-5216-3_2, © The Author(s) 2013

the consequences. This attribution problem enables attackers to launch large-scale cyber attacks with a comparably low risk of being held responsible for the attack.

A common goal of ongoing cyber attacks is to gain access to the targeted system. If the attack is successful, the attacker may perform any task that is possible for a regular user. In the worst case, the attacker may even gain the permission to perform restricted operations, which are only allowed for system administrators. These escalated permissions are commonly used to spy on the attacked user or steal sensitive data, like online banking credentials or credit card information. These malicious activities also not exclusively target the compromised systems themselves, but may target further systems as well. They can be used for example to gain access to additional systems, but also to hinder these systems from operating normally. Attackers perform these attacks for example to harm the operator of the targeted system respectively the according business or organization. This may be also accompanied by blackmailing attempts, forcing the victim to pay money in order to stop the attacks [1].

Instead of manually performing malicious activities on compromised hosts, attackers commonly manipulate the victim's system by secretly installing malicious programs. This so-called malware is then able to autonomously perform malicious activities as predefined by the attacker. Regardless of the concrete activities, their effect is based on the amount of compromised hosts in many cases. As an example, stealing banking credentials from a multitude of compromised systems may obviously result in higher revenues for the attacker. Consequentially, cyber criminals automated the process of compromising remote hosts in order to multiply their capabilities by orders of magnitude. Classic forms of malware like computer worms were thus able to autonomously spread over networks and perform predefined malicious activities on successfully attacked hosts.

A major drawback of this classic malware is that there is no way to interfere with running malware instances. If malware authors for example detect bugs in their software, there is no easy way to update already infected systems. Furthermore, there is no way to receive status information on demand or to adjust programmed malicious activities. In order to eliminate these shortcomings, malware authors added hidden communication channels allowing them to communicate with all infected systems. These so-called botnets also combine several classical malware functions, which makes them a general-purpose weapon to launch cyber attacks. The term botnet is generally used to describe a group of interconnected malicious programs that can be commanded over the Internet in order to perform various malicious tasks. The entire botnet can be controlled from a single machine by utilizing differently sophisticated connection architectures. In contrast to other kinds of malware, botnets don't carry out predefined attacks, but wait for according commands. These characteristics make botnets rather unpredictable, since they are able to completely change their behavior within a short time. Single botnets can furthermore contain more than a million of infected systems [2], which enable the commander to perform attacks on a multitude of systems simultaneously. Accessing a huge amount of systems from a single point and the ability dynamically react on individual circumstances makes this kind of malware posing an outstanding threat to any modern computer system.

In order to infect new systems, recent botnets also no longer exclusively rely on vulnerable services running on targeted hosts that can be directly attacked from the Internet. Instead, there are multiple other attack vectors, e.g., removable media or malicious documents. The advantage of these mediums is that it is even possible to attack computer systems, which are not connected to the Internet at all. More commonly, these attack vectors can be used to infect firewalled systems or systems within local networks that cannot be attacked from the Internet directly. This also poses a special threat to secured networks, which are a valuable target for cyber criminals. Various studies have shown that for example many employees attach private devices to their corporate network disregarding individual security policies [3, 4]. As a result, botnets are able to successfully infiltrate those secured networks for example by using removable media. By utilizing all of these attack vectors, including the Internet and removable media, it is possible to target almost any computer system operated today.

The actual purpose of an individual botnet may particularly depend on the attacker's intention. One of the most common motivations for operating botnets is generating revenue. Botnets monetize in many ways, for example by selling captured information on the black market. As an example, stolen credit card information is commonly sold in bulk for less than ten cents per credit card number [2]. To get a further impression, banking credentials were sold ranging from $10 to US$700 [5], depending on the account balance. These kinds of botnets are commonly developed, operated and also distributed by groups of organized crime [6]. However, there are also individual criminals using botnets for commercially motivated attacks. Beside these commercially oriented botnets, botnets also occur in political and military context. According groups do not primarily aim to generate revenue from their activities, but try to reach nonmonetary goals. A common motivation is to capture classified information in order to obtain a political or military advantage over possible counterparties [7]. In this context, highly specialized botnets have been discovered in the recent past, which are likely to be carried out by entire countries [8, 9]. In contrast to most commercially oriented botnets, which tend to have no special requirements on the attacked host, those botnets commonly affect carefully chosen hosts only. Beside these presumed governmental attacks, individuals may also utilize botnets by political means. In this case, individuals or political groups use botnet attacks as some sort of protest, which is one manifestation of so-called hacktivism. The use of botnets in context of hacktivism occurred in an unprecedented large scale in 2007, where criminals successfully launched denial of service attacks against various Estonian institutions [10]. Even if the case could not be solved with absolute certainty by today, it was most likely a reaction to the moving of a Soviet war memorial. Furthermore, individual autonomous groups like Anonymous or LulzSec use botnets for fun or to uphold their own interests. In 2010 for example, Anonymous used a voluntary botnet to launch an extensive denial of service attack against PayPal as a reaction to PayPal's decision to stop processing donations for Wikileaks [1, 4, 11, 12].

In Sect. 2, this article gives an insight into the technical details of current malware and botnet technologies. It is explained, how malicious programs manage to infect a victim's system and how default countermeasures are circumvented.

Focusing on botnet technologies, their architecture is discussed in detail. This includes the organization of a multitude of systems within a botnet and how these botnets try to mitigate the impact of various countermeasures. Additionally, common protocols used for communication are discussed as well as the necessary steps for malicious programs needed to join the communication network after having a vulnerable system infected.

Section 3 describes the current state in botnet developments. Due to the commercialization of botnets, they are developed by professionals as part of a malicious economy. Bots are sold in form of construction kits, allowing even unskilled criminals to create their own customized botnet. The long-lasting development of botnet technologies has also resulted in a multitude of tools and code samples that are freely available and can be used to develop new botnets with little effort. Furthermore, the spreading techniques of current botnets are discussed as well as the platforms they are targeting.

Subsequent to the description of botnet technologies and the current situation, Sect. 4 describes how to detect botnets in the first place and how to gather more information out them. The necessary actions to effectively combat existing botnets can be grouped into techniques that are used to gather information about a botnet on the one hand and the actual countermeasures on the other hand. This section therefore starts with a description of current approaches used to detect botnets. Different approaches used to gather additional information about the detected botnet are discussed subsequently. This information can then be used to develop and apply customized countermeasures. To analyze a botnet's activity, current techniques to track active botnets are described accordingly. Additionally, it is possible to apply approaches to detect infected machines of individual botnets to get information about the botnet's spreading. Hence, corresponding techniques that are practically used today are described in this section.

When the needed information about specific botnets has been gathered, it is possible to develop and apply individual countermeasures. Therefore, various existing approaches to combat existing botnets are described in Sect. 5. These approaches can be divided into three groups, namely preventing new infections, mitigating existing botnets and minimizing their profit. To permanently defeat the botnet phenomenon, an integrated approach is needed requiring various technical and non-technical measures. Effectively combating botnets for example requires an extensive cooperation of all parties involved as well as an according political framework. Notwithstanding these complex requirements, this article focuses on the technical level. Therefore, a first step is to prevent computer systems from being infected. This is necessary, to slow down the spreading of active botnets and to prevent botnets from reinfecting systems that have been disinfected. This can be done by securing computer systems on the one hand, but also by educating end users on the other hand. The second level of combating botnets is to eliminate currently active botnets by disinfecting according systems. Finally yet importantly, the possible profit of botnets can be reduced to make botnets less attractive for cyber criminals. There exist various approaches for each group of countermeasures. In this section, we give an overview on these approaches and discuss each approach in detail.

2 Fundamentals

The vast majority of current cyber attacks related to cyber crime utilize malicious programs or malware [13]. Malware however is not a new invention of cyber criminals. The first malware for MS DOS called Brain already appeared in 1986 [14], long times before cyber crime in its current form occurred. However, brain was already able to actively prevent its detection, which is still done by current malware. Even if current malware occasionally uses more sophisticated technologies, the basic concept of spreading and hiding still remains. Brain autonomously spread via diskettes and contains no further malicious functionality than showing a short message, telling the user that his system has been infected. It also shows the address and phone numbers of the originators, so the victim could call them for vaccination. The intention was to identify people who copied protected software, since the virus was spread on purpose alongside with pirated software by the originators [15]. It did not take long though until first malware variants with more destructive potential appeared in the wild. As soon as 1987, the Lehigh virus was detected, which completely overwrites the data stored on the victim machines hard disk [16].

Also if Lehigh and other following destructive malware already caused a noteworthy amount of economic damage in the late eighties, they still do not correspond to today's cyber crime. Early malware was developed by unorganized individuals as a proof of concept or to demonstrate individual programming skills. In contrast, today's malware is largely developed to server particular purposes, as for example generating revenue. Cyber attackers can therefore revert to a large amount of public available code samples that can be used to create new botnets. Even the entire source code of existing botnets is available on the Internet, allowing even less skilled hackers to create individual and customized botnets. Furthermore, so-called construction kits can be used to individually create customized branches of existing malware. These construction kits are developed by organized groups of high skilled professionals as part of a malicious underground economy. In the course this commercially developed malware, these construction kits are licensed to customers as any regular software, sometimes even with day and night phone support. Despite these commercial off-the-shelf botnets, particular botnets are still developed and operated by groups of professionals. These botnets are developed with considerable effort and pose a huge threat to targeted computer systems.

The entire evolution of malware was heavily influenced by the growing use of the Internet. The Internet not only offers malware completely new ways to infect vulnerable systems but also provides malware with an easy way to communicate. Therefore, malware was able to communicate with each other on the one hand and with the originator on the other. The gained ability to communicate enables malware for example to directly send information from the infected machine back to the originator. This is rather elegant, especially compared to Brain, which tried to get the users of infected machines to actually call the originator by phone. Being able to communicate also offers the possibility to send information the other way round, namely from the originator to the malware. The originator was now able to instruct the malware, in order to react on individual circumstances. The potential of this capability can be illustrated by the example of CodeRed in 2001 [17]. CodeRed was a so-called self-spreading malware or computer worm, referred to the fact that it was able to autonomously infect vulnerable systems, but lacks the ability to communicate. It was programmed to launch a denial of service attack against the website of the White House. Therefore, it was instructed to frequently contact the corresponding IP address 7 days a month. Unfortunately from the author's perspective, the attack was recognized at an early stage. As a result, the IP address of the website was changed, rendering the attacks unsuccessful. If the originator would have had an option to just change the attacks target, he might have accomplished his mission.

Therefore, today's malware is often equipped with a hidden communication channel, allowing it to send and receive information to or from its originator. This communication channel can be used to send current status information directly from the malware to the originator or to transfer captured information from the infected machines. Furthermore, the communication channel can be used to send orders from the originator to the infected machines. The malware is therefore able to interpret the received orders and to act accordingly. Thus, the malware can be used to perform various malicious activities and is able to react on individual events. Since this kind of malware typically waits for incoming orders and reports the result back, it is referred to as robot or *bot*. A group of interconnected bots is referred to as *botnet* analogously. First botnets where discovered in 1999, namely Sub7 and Pretty Park [18]. Both where equipped with an IRC based communication channel, allowing them to receive orders over the Internet. Since the occurrence of this first and rather simple botnets, large numbers of new botnets appeared and became increasingly sophisticated.

In the following section, the technical details of botnets and malware in general are discussed. Beginning with a description of common obfuscation techniques and different types of malware, an overview on different technologies used by malware to infect new systems and hide from antivirus technologies is given. Furthermore, the communication protocols and network architectures used by botnets will be outlined. Additionally, different kinds of attacks commonly carried out by botnets are listed.

2.1 Malware

Malicious software, or malware for short, is one of the major threats for computer systems today. It has evolved from rare and rather simple specimens to a huge amount of highly sophisticated programs. In 2010 alone, Symantec has registered more than 286 million different copies of malware [2]. Beside this magnitude, current malware also uses state of the art technologies to mitigate various antivirus solutions. These technologies are directly related to the vast amount of different malware that can be observed today as described in the following.

2.1.1 Obfuscation

Malware commonly uses various kinds of techniques in order to mitigate antivirus solutions. Therefore, malware may try to apply active countermeasures, for example disabling antivirus solutions. Another approach used by malware is to passively prevent their detection by deceiving antivirus solutions. This is commonly done for example by obfuscating the malware binary in a way, in which it can no longer be detected.

A common measure to prevent individual systems from being infected by malware is by using antivirus software. This software commonly relies on signatures that somehow describe the content of a malicious program. The advantage of this approach is that malware can be detected by using a minimum amount of system resources. Every program is statically checked if it matches a set of signatures right before its execution. Since malware developers anticipate this procedure, they try to manipulate the binary representation of the malware without actually changing the program flow. This can be done for example by adding code to malware, which is not executed at all, or does not affect the rest of the program. Analogously, various instructions without any effect can be merged into the code. Other commonly used techniques try to manipulate the entire code by packing or encrypting the malware. To ensure that the malware is still able to run on regular systems, an unpacking or decrypting routine is added to the program, which undoes previous modifications as soon as the program is loaded. Thus, antivirus programs are unable to detect suspicious code sequences with the help of static signatures. By utilizing these so-called *polymorphing* techniques, it is not longer possible, to easily recognize different copies of one and the same malware. Every registered malware is detected as a new malware instead, which leads to the huge amount of copies that can be observed today.

2.1.2 Classification

Since many different kinds of malware with different functionalities exist, their functionality can be assigned to various classes. Despite these differences, all kinds of malware also share some common characteristics. Since most users would not install malicious programs on purpose, malware is always installed on computer systems without the owner's consent. The most prominent classes of malware functionalities are described below. However most of the current malware cannot be assigned to exactly one class, but has characteristics of multiple classes. Hence, these classes are used to characterize the functionality of various different kinds of malware.

Virus: The computer virus is probably the most prominent kind of malware. However, this does not imply that computer viruses actually are the most common kind of malware but refers to the fact that both terms are often used synonymously. Originally, the term computer virus is used for a special kind of self-replicating malware. A computer virus is a parasitic piece of software, which injects itself for example into another executable program. If this program is launched, the viral code is launched too and thus able to perform various malicious activities. To infect further systems, an infected file has to be transmitted to another system, where it has to be executed by the user in order to infect the system. To enforce the transmission to other systems, computer viruses may not only infect local files but also files on removable media or mounted network shares.

Worm: Whereas viruses rely on user interaction to infect new machines, computer worms have automated this task by actively spreading over the network, e.g., the Internet. Therefore, computer worms automatically scan the network for vulnerable systems. If such a system is detected it can automatically be infected by exploiting software vulnerabilities in the operating system or user applications.

Trojan Horse: Trojan horses use a rather different approach to infect new systems, namely by deceiving users about its functionality. Trojan horses masquerade as useful software, providing some legitimate functionality. If the Trojan horse is installed or executed, the embedded malicious functionality is also executed. For the user, only the benign functionality is visible, which keeps the user from getting suspicious.

Rootkit: A rootkit is a collection of malicious tools with a specific functionality, which is commonly used by other kinds of malware. Rootkits are used to hide various malicious activities like malicious files, open networking sockets or running processes on the infected machines. This prevents other malware for example from being detected by antivirus software or the user. To perform these tasks, rootkits commonly require administrator or root privileges on the infected systems. Since rootkits may reside in the operating systems core components, removing them can be a difficult task, which may require completely reinstalling the operating system.

Dropper: Beside rootkits, droppers are another step into the modularization of today's malware. By using droppers, the spreading routine of a malware can be separated from the malicious activity. Therefore, droppers are used to infect a system in the first place and install other malware afterwards. Separating the spreading routine from a malware brings more flexibility since the dropper can be easily replaced if it is for example detected by antivirus software. Furthermore, using a dropper ensures that the latest version of a malware is installed on all infected machines. This can be done, if the actual malware is downloaded from a central server onto the infected systems. Updating the malware on this server therefore results in the dropper installing the updated malware.

2.2 Botnets

Botnets consist of a particular kind of malware, the so-called *bots* or *drones*. These drones combine malicious functionalities of other malware classes into one general-purpose weapon for cyber attackers. Since bots are able to perform a multitude of malicious activities on demand, they are rather unpredictable. In contrast to other malware, botnets are extremely flexible and are able to dynamically react on external events, which makes them particularly dangerous. Botnets can be used for example to extract valuable information from large amounts of infected systems simultaneously or to perform other malicious activities as described in Sect. 2.2.1. The decisive factor that separates a bot from other kinds of malware is, however, not the utilized spreading routine or malicious functionality but the hidden communication channel. This communication channel allows individual bots to communicate with each other and their operator. In this context, the operator of a botnet is commonly referred to as *botmaster* or *botherder.* The term botnet is used to describe an entire network of bots, which share a common communication channel.

The communication channel between the botmaster and the individual bots is used to transmit data from the infected machines to the botmaster, as well as to send commands from the botmaster to the individual bots. In contrast to other kinds of malware, botnets actually require commands from the botmaster in order to perform malicious activities. The different bots can then process the received commands automatically. Therefore, every bot supports a fixed set of predefined tasks that can be executed on demand. To overcome the shortcoming of a fixed and limited instruction set, many current botnets support update commands. By using this command, existing bots can be easily replaced by a new version with an extended instruction set. This feature not only enables bots to perform almost arbitrary tasks on the infected machines, but also offers the opportunity to perform maintenance updates. The update functionality can be utilized for example to perform bug fixes or to protect the botnet from individual takeover attempts.

2.2.1 Frauds

Beside this generic command, botnets can support various commands to perform individual malicious activities, which are commonly commercially motivated. These frauds are commonly offered as a service from botnet operators, which are part of the botnet economy. Like botmasters are able to purchase entire botnets from professional and organized teams of developers, botmasters can provide individual malicious activities on the black market.

A common fraud, which is supported by most botnets, is the distribution of unsolicited mass mails or Spam. Therefore, the bot is commonly provided with lists of email addresses and a so-called spam-template. This template contains the actual content of the spam-mail as well as a schema, which defines how parts of the content can be randomized to complicate signature-based detection used by spam filters. Botnets like Waledac were observed to send out about 150,000 spam-mails per day from individual infected machines [19]. Overall, spam-emails are estimated to account for 80–90 % of all globally sent emails [20]. Since the distribution of spam emails is offered as a service from botnet operators, spam can provide a particular source of income. The total amount of revenue that can be generated by offering this service can be estimated by considering spam rental pricing on the black market. Using this service may cost botnet customers from US$70 for a few thousand spam messages up to US$1000 for tens of millions [21]. The intention for using this service can be different, but commonly is to advertise various products in order to generate revenue as well.

Another commonly observed intention is to infect further machines by either directly including a malicious attachment or containing a link to a malicious website. Additionally, so-called phishing emails are used to steal passwords or other private information from receivers by using social engineering techniques. Another form of spamming is search engine optimization (SEO) spamming. Many search engines rank web pages according to the number of incoming links from external web pages. Therefore, bots post links to individual pages for example to bulletin boards, in order to get these pages ranked higher in search results. Similar to other forms of spamming, this service can be sold on the black market to generate revenue.

A second commonly observed malicious task that is supported by bots is launching distributed denial of service (DDoS) attacks. These attacks are also commonly commercially motivated and are therefore often observed in conjunction with blackmail attempts. Thus, potential victims are extorted to pay money in order to prevent their systems from being attacked [22]. DDoS attacks are used to sabotage a remote system in order to prevent it from being accessed by regular users. Therefore, botnets commonly overwhelm the targeted system with connection requests from various distributed machines. Consequently, the targeted system is busy processing the botnets request and no longer able to process requests of regular users. Since it may be difficult to distinguish a botnets request from a regular user's request, it can be rather complicated to defend endangered systems from this kind of attack.

Whereas the previous two examples of malicious botnet activities focus on attacking external machines, botnets can also be used to attack the infected system itself. As bots are executed like any regular application on the infected machines, they also have access to same data. Moreover, bots are commonly executed with administrator privileges, which give them unrestricted access to every data, resource or process on the infected system. These privileges are used for example to intercept keystrokes on the infected machines by applying a so-called keylogger. This allows the bot to even access data that is not stored permanently on the disk, like passwords entered in login forms. To protect online banking accounts from botnets, transactions are additionally protected for example by one-time passwords. As a result, botnets try to manipulate online banking transactions directly in the browser, by secretly changing the recipient as a transaction takes place [23]. After the transaction is completed, the bot rewrites the list of completed transactions to prevent the victim of becoming suspicious. To circumvent two-factor authentication, botnets like ZeuS manipulate login forms directly in the browser by adding input fields for all security answers [24].

The preceding frauds are just a few examples for common malicious botnet activities. Another common example is virtually clicking on advertisements from the infected machines. This so-called click-fraud directly generates revenue for the one displaying the advertisement on his website. Botmasters can also be paid to install other malware on the infected machines of their botnet. This activity is mostly referred to as pay-per-install. Moreover, infected machines of a botnets can be used to host various services that are needed to operate a botnet by providing command-and-control infrastructure for example. Beyond these examples, many more malicious activities are possible. Since botnets commonly include some form of update mechanism, these activities can always be changed to meet current requirements.

2.2.2 Attack Vectors

A special kind of malicious activity commonly supported by botnets is infecting remote systems in order to integrate them into the botnet. During the evolution of botnets, the used techniques have become increasingly sophisticated and highly efficient. As a result, botnet infections are no longer limited to outdated or poorly secured systems but also include highly secured systems in protected environments. A look at the recent past shows, that botnets like Conficker managed to infect hundreds of systems within military networks in Germany, France and the United Kingdom [25]. Since the operation of Conficker is most likely commercially motivated, the infection of those machines could be considered as collateral damage. In contrast, politically motivated espionage botnets like GhostNet especially targeted classified systems in various governments [8].

To infect new systems, many botnets try to exploit software vulnerabilities in order to execute custom code on the targeted system. Flaws in the processing of input data, like uncaught buffer overflows, may allow the attacking system to inject code sequences into the process memory of a vulnerable application. As a result, the injected code is executed in the context of the vulnerable application and therefore with the same permissions. This so-called *shellcode* can now be used to download and install a copy of the attacking bot on the targeted system to complete the infection process. Therefore, highly sophisticated self-spreading malware like Stuxnet takes advantage of even multiple 0-day exploits (which are exploits for previously unknown vulnerabilities) to gain access to vulnerable systems [26]. Since software vendors or security companies do not know the exploited vulnerability in advance, there are no patches to protect affected systems. It should be noted here, that even if Stuxnet shows several characteristics of a classic botnet, it is still able to operate completely autonomously to carry out a predefined mission. It is therefore debatable, whether Stuxnet should actually be referred to as botnet or not.

A classic strategy in exploiting software vulnerabilities is to exploit public services of a remote system, which can be accessed over the network. These services can either be offered directly by the operating system, like RPC on windows machines, or by server applications like web or database servers. Vulnerable services may allow an attacker to directly gain access to the system and install malicious software in background. This approach has already been used by the

Morris worm in 1988, which is considered to be the first malware spreading autonomously over the network [16]. Another approach to directly gain access to a remote system is by exploiting services that are protected by weak passwords. Botnets like Conficker automatically try to spread for example via network shares by simply trying commonly used passwords [27]. Another interesting approach on how remote systems can be directly infected is by using vulnerabilities or back-doors in other malware. This so-called worm-riding is for example used by *SdBot* variants, which scan for *MyDoom* or *Bagle* backdoors [28]. The major benefit of attacking a remote system directly over the network is that vulnerable systems can be infected without requiring any user interaction. They can therefore be infected, without the owner noticing.

Attacking a remote system directly over the network however requires the vulnerable service to be accessible for the attacking system. This reduces the amount of potential victims by firewalled systems or systems behind NAT-enabled routers. Furthermore, the attacked system has to be online while the attack takes place. To overcome these shortcomings, many botnets try to exploit vulnerabilities in client applications like web browsers or document viewers. Therefore, malicious code is embedded for example into websites or documents, which are then actively downloaded by the victim system. To enforce this process, malicious documents or links to malicious websites can be emailed to the victim. Malicious code can also be placed on benign websites for example by using cross side scripting (XSS) techniques. Infecting benign websites to deliver malicious code can also be auto-mated by botnets, which has been shown for example by the *Gumblar* botnet in 2009 [29]. If a user visits an infected website with a vulnerable browser, his system gets infected in background which is why these kinds of attacks are also called drive-by attacks. In these scenarios, the victim downloads the malicious code when it is online and bypasses network based security mechanisms like fire-walls. If the malicious content is opened with a vulnerable client application, a security flaw can be exploited to execute custom code on the victim system which is then used to install and launch a copy of the attacking bot. Depending on the quality of the used attack, the whole process is completely invisible to the user.

In the recent past, software vendors have developed increasingly sophisti-cated techniques to complicate the exploitation of security flaws. Furthermore, it can require a considerable effort to detect security flaws in the first place and to develop a reliable exploit. Nevertheless, there is no guarantee that developed exploits can be successfully used to infect potential victim machines for exam-ple due to different patch-levels. As a result, various botnets try to infect remote machines without exploiting any vulnerabilities or security flaws at all. Since users will not infect their systems voluntarily, botnets trick users into manually install-ing a copy of the attacking bot. Therefore, malicious executables can be masquer-aded as potential harmless document or vCard by using the appropriate icon and hidden file extension. Another example is to convince the user that the malicious file is actually benign and contains some interesting functionality, which is com-monly referred to as social engineering. This technique has been successfully used by the *Storm* botnet in 2007 to infect more than a million of systems [30]. Storm therefore uses spam emails to redirect users to websites containing a download link to a copy of Storm which is advertised for example as a utility to display digital postcards [31].

Beside attack vectors relying on Internet connections, botnets can also utilize removable media to propagate from one system to another. Since USB flash drives are widespread and commonly connected to different machines, they offer an attack vector especially to target machines without Internet connectivity. Therefore, the attack is stored on a flash drive in combination with a copy of the attacking bot. If the flash drive is then connected to a vulnerable system, software vulnerabilities or security flaws can be exploited to infect the system. The concept of utilizing removable media to infect remote system was already used by *Brain* in 1986 [14] and is still used by modern malware like *Stuxnet* [26] or *Conficker* [27].

A rather different approach of infecting new systems is by using another botnet. In contrast to other attack vectors, the actual infection is not done by the spreading botnet itself but with the help of another botnet. Many botnets are capable of installing additional malware on the infected system, which can be offered as a service to other botnets. This so-called pay-per-install offers the opportunity to selectively infect a predefined amount of machines. Depending on the geographic location of the targeted system, prices can range from US$13 to US$150 per 1000 installs [32]. The second benefit of this approach is that it offers a new kind of flexibility. Particular botnets can focus on the infection of machines whereas other botnets can focus on malicious activities and use pay-per-install for spreading.

2.2.3 Architectures

After having a multitude of machines infected, they have to be organized within a communication network in order to receive commands. This so-called command-and-control infrastructure organizes the communication between control entities on the one hand and the infected machines on the other. The design of this infrastructure can be crucial for the operation of a botnet since it has to meet certain requirements. Large botnets may need load-balancing techniques in order to prevent the command and control server from collapsing due to a large amount of simultaneous requests. Furthermore, the architecture has to be robust against potential countermeasures to maintain the botnet's operability as long as possible. During the evolution of botnets, cyber criminals have developed various techniques and architectures to reliably organize a botnet's communication infrastructure. These particular approaches differ in complexity while providing a different set of features. Thus, different architectures have their individual assets and drawbacks from the botmasters perspective, which is why many different approaches can be observed today.

A classic and rather simple command-and-control infrastructure is a centralized or star-shaped infrastructure, which is illustrated in Fig. 1. In this setup, each bot of a particular botnet connects to one central C&C server to receive new commands. Therefore, the botmaster is able to command all connected

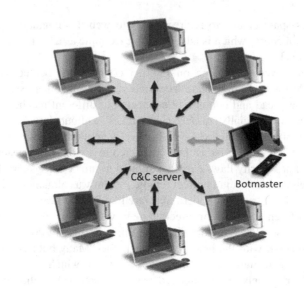

Fig. 1 Star-shaped botnet topology

bots simultaneously and receive response data directly from the bots. Since this approach is easy to implement and to deploy, it is still widely used by today's botnets. A major drawback of a centralized architecture is the lack of redundancy, which makes the C&C server a single point of failure. In case of a failure or successful takedown attempt, individual bots are no longer able to receive new commands from the botmaster. A common example for a centralized C&C architecture is the use of the IRC protocol. In this architecture, bots join a dedicated chat room and interpret received chat messages as commands.

A slightly more complicated C&C infrastructure uses multiple servers to create redundancies and eliminate a single point of failure. Another advantage of this approach is that it provides some kind of load balancing. This can be achieved for example by using DNS to address the C&C server and registering the IP addresses of the different servers for the according domain name. These IP addresses are then be delivered alternately to distribute requests to all servers. Even though this architecture provides more resistance against potential takedown attempts, it is more complex to operate. Furthermore, the usage of DNS would provide a new single point of failure without the use of any additional techniques.

To create a more resilient C&C infrastructure, control entities or servers can be arranged hierarchically, as depicted in Fig. 2. In this hierarchy, the lowest level actually controls the infected machines whereas the highest level is directly instructed by the botmaster. Intermediate layers only communicate with the next higher or lower layer. Individual bots for instance do not need to know about the actual command-and-control server but only about the lowest server layer. To send commands to the infected machines, the botmaster only needs to instruct the highest layer, from where new commands are propagated down in the hierarchy to the individual bots. This provides load balancing and anonymization of the actual

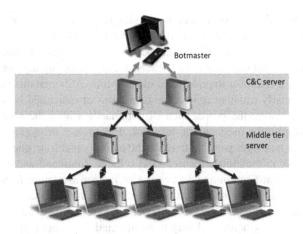

Fig. 2 Multi-tier architecture

Fig. 3 Peer-to-peer architecture

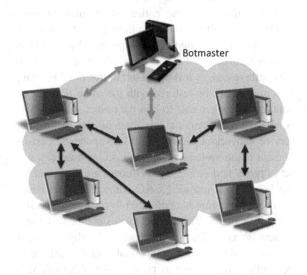

C&C server. Furthermore, the entire botnet can be easily fragmented into different groups, to perform different tasks on different machines. It is also more difficult to successfully apply takedown attempts since it may be necessary to takedown an entire layer at once to sustainably disrupt the botnet's communication. On the other hand, hierarchical botnet architectures are much more complex to develop and operate than simple centralized architectures. Furthermore, delays in the communication can occur due to the use of multiple relay servers.

Although multi-server architectures provide a resilient communication infrastructure, they still rely on a relatively small amount of servers that could potentially be fought by botnet counter-parties. To get rid of any kind of centralized server components, botnets like Storm utilize *peer-to-peer* protocols for command and control communication [33]. In peer-to-peer topologies (Fig. 3) bots communicate with each other and propagate commands through the network. To give new orders to the botnet, the botmaster can just join the peer-to-peer network and send new commands to an individual bot. Since the botmaster can connect to any bot to send out new commands, it is almost impossible to identify him. Although this kind of architecture is particularly resistant against the take down of individual bots, it is rather complex. Furthermore, the propagation of commands within the network can be slow. Depending on the used routing protocol, peer-to-peer networks can get fragmented, i.e., it is no longer possible to reach the entire botnet from one single bot.

A crucial task in creating a resilient and reliable command-and-control infrastructure is the identification and addressing of the infrastructure from individual bots. Every time a bot is started on an infected machine, it has to identify the C&C infrastructure in order to join the botnet and receive new commands. Since the entire C&C infrastructure is likely to be affected by botnet countering organizations, it has to be flexible to compensate the loss of individual components. Therefore, the addressing of the C&C infrastructure has to be flexible as well to remain control over the entire set of infected machines. Furthermore, the rally mechanism itself has to be resilient against potential countermeasures.

Directly addressing C&C components by their IP addresses is a very simple kind of rally mechanism that has already been used by early botnets. Although it requires only little resources it is prone to failures or takedown attempts. If a C&C component fails and cannot be restored with the same IP address, bots using this C&C component are no longer able to join the botnet and are therefore lost from the botmaster's perspective. To overcome this shortcoming, various botnets rely on so-called fast-flux service networks to contact C&C components. Fast-flux service networks utilize the domain name system to redirect C&C connection attempts to a constantly changing set of proxy nodes. These proxy nodes are then used to exchange information between the bot and the intended C&C component. To create a fast-flux service network, a fixed domain name is configured to resolve to the IP addresses of a subset of available proxy nodes. These IP addresses are than frequently changed to the IP addresses of new proxy nodes available, which is why this technique is also referred to as IP-fluxing. In this scenario, individual bots that can be reached from the Internet could be configured to server as proxy nodes. Alternately, fast-flux services can be rented from other botnets. The major benefit of this approach is, that it is resistant against the takedown of used C&C components. Since proxy nodes are constantly replaced, the takedown of individual proxy nodes has only temporary impact on the entire rally mechanism. Furthermore, proxy nodes can be flexibly configured to arbitrary C&C components. The proxy nodes also provide a certain degree of anonymity for other C&C components since they are not addressed directly by individual bots. A major drawback of the approach is that it heavily relies on a certain domain name to be available, in order to successfully create a connection between bots and C&C components. It is therefore necessary for the domain name to remain available regardless of potential abuse reports or reminders. Those so-called bulletproof domain names can be rented completely anonymously for around US$100 per year from dubious hosting companies [12]. However, the used domain name remains a single point of failure.

To be independent from a single domain name, domain-fluxing uses dynamically generated domain names in order to address C&C components. Therefore, each bot frequently calculates a set of domain names, depending on a variable input value. Within a particular time frame, this input value has to be equal for each bot in order to ensure that each calculates an identical set of domain names. Therefore, a possible input value can be the current date, as used by Conficker [34], or a popular website like Google or Twitter trends [35]. When a bot has calculated a set of domain names with respect to a particular initialization value, it tries to resolve every generated domain name in order to contact the intended C&C component. If the C&C component cannot be reached by any of the generated domain names, the bot can just retry with a new initialization value within the next time frame. Since the botmaster knows the used domain name generation algorithm, he can anticipate the generated domain names for a particular time frame. He can therefore register one of the generated domains for a particular time frame in order to send new commands to the botnet. Hence, this approach is independent from single domain names and is further resistant against the takedown of individual C&C components.

3 Botnets: The Current Situation

Since the occurrence of first botnets in 1999, they have evolved to communicational networks of highly sophisticated malicious utilities. Whereas early botnets were created by individuals as a demonstration of own skills to be honored by the community, the motivation for current is different. Current botnets are professionally developed by a mature industry, which is part of an entire malware economy [5]. Developers, as part of the malware industry, are paid as any regular employee and recruited by online advertisements [36]. As a result, commercial off-the-shelf botnets can be bought in form of construction kits from dubious developers or malware gangs [37]. Various botnet construction kits like the so-called Aldi Bot can be bought on discount for about 5€ on underground forums [38]. Consequently, botnets are no longer solely operated by their developers, but also by potentially less skilled customers.

The customer of a botnet construction kit is then able, to create and control a customized botnet. This botnet can again be used to sell particular malicious services like the distribution of spam email or launching denial of service attacks. Additionally, data captured from the infected machines can be sold on the black market. Therefore, modern botmasters can be referred to as malicious service provides, which are just one part of the entire cyber crime ecosystem. To pay for botnet services, the botnet ecosystem also includes dedicated groups managing financial transfers of money. These groups therefore create special banking accounts or trick naive depositors to take part in transferring money between various bank accounts [39]. These so-called money mules were usually recruited with social engineering techniques, for example by job offers that include money transfers.

Since the source code of various bots is publicly available [40], it has become rather simple to create individual customized botnets. Only 3 months after the source code of the infamous ZeuS botnet has been leaked, the first new botnet based on this particular source code has been observed [41]. Other examples like AgoBot, whose source code has been published in 2003, has spawned more than 580 variants until 2007 [42]. Even though many active botnets are known, the total number of currently operating botnets can hardly be estimated. Beside the unknown number of not yet detected botnets, it can be tough to count botnets at all. Since botnets commonly utilize polymorphing techniques to manipulate their binary footprint, counting the total amount of unique bot samples only gives a less meaningful estimation. Instead, a commonly used metric to count active botnets is by counting according command-and-control servers. However, this approach may be affected from botnets using multiple C&C server, peer-to-peer botnets with no dedicated C&C server or C&C infrastructures in which the C&C server is only deployed on demand. By using this approach, about 5500 different botnets were observed for the beginning of 2011 by individual institutions [43]. During this period, botnet infections could be detected from more than 200,000 unique IP addresses, which is also just a rough estimation on the actual amount of infected machines. In contrast, other sources claim to have detected more than 10 million individual infected systems [44]. Moreover, it could be observed that more than 35 % of the infected IP addresses were infected by at least two different botnets. It should further be noted that beside the challenges in measuring the amount of botnets and according infected machines, it can be difficult to get objective numbers. These numbers are commonly published by companies providing security solutions. Since cyber security is a huge market, these companies commonly have an incentive to exaggerate the number of infected systems.

In the recent past, the size of a botnet has also been the most significant indicator to measure the threat posed by individual botnets. This is however a very general observation, which does not take the purpose of individual botnets into account. In case of denial-of-service attacks, the available bandwidth for example is more important than the pure amount of infected machines. Moreover, most servers can be successfully attacked by several hundreds of infected machines [45]. As a result, larger botnets are not necessarily more dangerous for individual servers on the Internet. The threat posed by information stealing botnets on the other hand depends on the kind of the infected machines. GhostNet for example infected less than 1300 systems, but up to 30 % of these systems could be considered as high-value targets in ministries of foreign affairs or embassies [8]. Recent studies therefore suggest to take these factors into account as well, in order to create a more realistic estimation on the threat posed by individual botnets [46].

Whereas the vast majority of botnets still target windows platforms only, an increasing amount of botnets has started to target other platforms as well. Due to the increasing market share of Mac OS X, researchers have detected the first botnet targeting Mac OS X in 2009 [47]. In 2011, a Java based botnet has been detected that is able to infect windows platforms as well as Mac OS X and Unix systems [48]. In the recent years, botnets have also increasingly focused on mobile devices. Whereas 31 malware families were known to target mobile devices in 2006, the number of mobile bots has increased up to 153 families with more than 1000 variants in 2010 [49]. Infamous botnets like ZeuS for example can be observed to start infecting mobile devices alongside to common end user computer systems [50]. This enables the bot to intercept mTANs that were sent to mobile devices in order to approve a financial transaction made from an infected computer system. Furthermore mobile devices offer new potentials for malicious activities like the manipulation of wireless payments or sending SMS to premium numbers.

To infect new systems, malware of all kinds heavily relies on user interactions. Recent studies show, that almost half of all infections where manually triggered by users [51]. Therefore, users are encouraged for example by emails or other documents to manually install particular software that contains the malicious code. This approach is much more reliable than the exploitation of security flaws, since it does not rely on specific software versions or path levels. As a result, less than 6 % of currently active malware uses software vulnerabilities in order to infect new systems. The most commonly used exploits target vulnerabilities in Java components, followed by HTML/JavaScript and operating system vulnerabilities [51]. These numbers are, however, based on one survey and may differ depending on the surveyed systems. The second most commonly used attack vector utilizes the AutoRun functionality to automatically execute malicious binaries on USB removable media. Conficker or Stuxnet use this attack for example in addition to web based attack vectors to increase the infection rate. In case of Stuxnet, it is also necessary to infect computer systems that are not connected to the Internet.

4 Analyzing the Threat

Current botnets are highly sophisticated tools that use complex techniques for communication. Furthermore, there are many different botnets that may use completely different technologies. This applies to the attack vectors, the C&C communication as well as to the binary itself. Therefore, there is no general-purpose method to analyze all currently active botnets, but a set of different tools and techniques. With the help of these tools, a lot of information about individual botnets has to be gathered, in order to efficiently apply custom countermeasures.

The following section therefore describes various techniques that can be applied to detect previously unknown botnets in the first place. These botnets can then be analyzed by using different techniques that are described subsequently in order to get detailed insight into the functionality of an individual botnet. These techniques can also be used to gather information on individual botnets that can be used to apply custom countermeasures. This information can further be used to track the activities of a botnet to get an insight into the botnets operation. Therefore, various tracking techniques are discussed in the following section. Detailed information on individual botnets can also be used to remotely identify infected machines within particular networks or the entire Internet. Several approaches that can be applied to identify infected machines of modern botnets are also discussed in the following section.

4.1 Detecting

Before any other kind of analysis technique can be applied, each botnet hast to be detected in the first place. A major challenge in this context is to detect previously unknown botnets. Therefore, it is not known a priori, which methods are for example used to infect other machines or how the bot behaves on infected systems. As a result, detection techniques are constantly adjusted to cope with current botnet technologies. Botnet authors on the other hand, improve their techniques to mitigate state-of-the-art detection techniques. This arms race has spawned various different detection techniques that are discussed in the following section.

In general, botnets can be detected based on three major characteristics. One common characteristic of many botnets is to autonomously infect new systems, which can be detected by observing the medium that is used to attack further systems or by observing potential victims. Another common characteristic, which is shared by all malware, is some form of malicious activity. Depending on the particular activity, this can be detected for example by analyzing network connections from likely infected hosts. A rather botnet specific characteristic is the use of a command-and-control channel used by the infected machines to receive orders from their botmaster. Since botnets rely on this communication by definition, they can always be detected by this characteristic in principle. Even though, botnets may disguise their communication, which makes it hard to detect them in practice. To detect a botnets communication, network traffic can be analyzed for certain C&C pattern. As a result, there is no general-purpose technique to detect previously unknown botnets, but a set of different approaches each with its own pros and cons.

4.1.1 Log File Analysis

Whenever a bot infects a new system, it commonly changes certain system files for example in order to ensure it gets loaded after the next reboot. Most modern operating systems protocol such activities in human readable files, the so-called *log files*. By analyzing these log files, unintended system file changes can be detected which may indicate a successful bot infection. Even though system log files are human readable, it can be complicated for non-professionals to separate intended and malicious activities apart. Therefore, tools like host-based intrusion detection systems (HIDS) constantly monitor log file changes to detect malicious behavior. If such a behavior is detected, the user can be automatically alarmed. The major benefit of this approach is that botnets are not detected by their used attack or binary footprint but by the effects of a successful infection. Since the used exploit does not need to be known in order to detect an infection, HIDS are able to detect even previously unknown botnets. However, this approach also comes with a major drawback. Botnet infections are detected after a successful infection, which provides the bot with the possibility to apply active countermeasures in order to prevent its detection. The bot could therefore shut down host-based security mechanisms or tamper with created log files.

Beside the evaluation of system log files, it is also possible to analyze log files created by certain applications. Particular examples for such log files are log files as created by firewalls. If botnets for example try to create a connection to their C&C server on a port that is blocked by the firewall, a log file entry is created. Therefore, many connection attempts can be registered that are blocked by the firewall may also indicate a bot infection. It is further possible to use firewall log files in order to detect the spreading behavior of botnets. If a bot tries to infect a system on a port that is blocked by the local firewall, this incident will be added to the firewall log files. By analyzing the according log files, it can be unveiled which systems have caused the registered attacks. This information is especially useful if both systems operate within the same authority, for example a corporate network. In this scenario, the infected machine can be localized directly to apply further measures.

A general drawback in log file analysis is that log files do not only contain information on incidents, but also a lot of other information. Consequentially, large amount of information has to be analyzed in order to detect certain incidents. Since incidents cannot be identified with certainty in all cases, this may lead to a rather large amount of false alarms or missed incidents compared to other detection techniques.

4.1.2 Antivirus

Host-based intrusion detection capabilities are also included in various modern *antivirus* solutions. In contrast to classic antivirus solutions that solely rely on pre-calculated signatures to recognize the binary footprint of previously known bot samples, modern versions feature a set of techniques to detect previously unknown samples as well. By the use of static heuristics, antivirus products are able to recognize the functionality of certain byte sequences. This information can give a brief overview on particular sequences of the malicious code and may indicate malicious behavior in analyzed samples of previously unknown bot samples. As an example, decryptor or unpacking stubs commonly used by botnets to obfuscate their binary footprint can be detected in various cases by static heuristics. To improve the detection rate for unknown botnets, various antivirus solutions also apply dynamic heuristics to suspicious files. Therefore, the execution of the binary is emulated in order to gain more detailed information on the runtime behavior. During the emulation, intended changes to the hosting system can be observed to detect presumed malicious behavior.

Both kinds of heuristics enable antivirus solutions to detect previously unknown botnets in general. However, there are also various drawbacks in using heuristics to detect malicious behavior. Static heuristics in the first place can be applied with low computational costs on the one hand but are rather unreliable on the other. Dynamic heuristics on the other hand are usually much slower than static heuristics and are still no guarantee that malicious samples can be detected. Since antivirus solutions are very common, botnet authors especially focus on deceiving antivirus heuristics to stay undetected.

4.1.3 Network Analysis

Instead of applying detection techniques directly on host systems, it is also possible to analyze the network traffic. By using this approach, it is possible to detect the spreading of botnets, their C&C communication and various malicious activities. This can be done either by reconstructing the data, which is send over the network, or by directly analyzing connection information. The latter can be done for example by observing communication anomalies that are likely to be caused by botnets. Reassembling data streams to inspect the data that is send over the network is a classic approach used by network-based intrusion detection systems (NIDS). This technique is also known as deep packet inspection, since the entire content of a network packet is analyzed. Therefore, NIDS simulate the according protocol stacks to reassemble received packets just like a regular communication endpoint. The reconstructed payload is then compared with a set of pre-calculated signatures to automatically identify various known malicious communication patterns or binary footprints. If the system is also able to interrupt malicious connections to prevent host systems from getting infected, it is also referred to as intrusion prevention system or IPS.

Since NIDS can be deployed apart from individual host systems, they do not have to operate on potentially infected machines. As a result, botnets can hardly apply active countermeasures to prevent their detection. Furthermore, it is possible to observe entire networks from one single machine. A major drawback of NIDS is the limited scalability in order to observe the entire communication of networks with high traffic loads. Furthermore, NIDS are only able to reconstruct non-encrypted network traffic. If botnets use encryption for example to contact their C&C server, the containing malicious communication pattern cannot be detected. On the other hand, malicious communication using unknown pattern cannot be detected at all. Botnets try to exploit this by using evasion techniques to conceal their communication in order to avoid certain pattern within their communication. A simple example for such so-called evasion techniques is splitting messages into multiple network packets. As a result, only small parts of known malicious pattern are contained within individual packets. Thus, the communication will not be detected by NIDS and the bot is not detected. This simple example will only work for NIDS that inspect individual packets separately, but there are also more complex evasion techniques to deal with NIDS performing network stream reassembly. Every operating system uses a slightly different protocol stack implementation with slightly different behavior. Therefore, one protocol stack implementation might accept certain types of malformed packets while they are discarded by other implementations. This can be exploited to insert packets into the communication that are accepted by the NIDS but discarded by the actual communication endpoint. On the other hand, it is possible to create packets that are only accepted by the communication endpoint. Both techniques can be used by botnets to prevent their communication from being detected by NIDS and thus, prevent their detection by this kind of detection mechanism. Another general aspect of analyzing the payload of network traffic is, that it might violate the users privacy. Thus, this kind of detection technique cannot be applied due to legal restrictions in various cases.

Instead of using pattern matching to detect previously known botnet communication, other approaches try to detect communication anomalies. These anomaly-based network intrusion detection systems (A-NIDS) exploit the fact that the communication of various botnets may differ from regular network traffic. As an example, Conficker infected systems use domain-fluxing to contact their C&C server. Therefore, every bot tries to resolve a set of randomly generated domain names, depending on the particular date. This procedure results in a multitude of domain-names that do not exist and thus cannot be resolved. If there are multiple infected machines within an observed network, this behavior can be observed from those machines as well. Having various machines within one network that fail to resolve a multitude of previously unused domain names can therefore be considered as irregular behavior. While this is a rather striking example of network anomalies, other botnet activities may be harder to detect. A-NIDSs therefore observe various network characteristics like used protocols, which systems communicate with each other or the network load of individual systems.

To define regular network communication, A-NIDSs commonly use some kind of training phase to initialize internal detection parameters. As a result, A-NIDSs are able to detect previously unknown botnets by their communication, if the communication differs from regular network communications in a sufficient level. This however requires the traffic to be benign during the initialization phase. If systems within the observed network were already infected, the malicious communication would be considered as regular and cannot be detected afterwards. This also applies if the communication used by a new botnet lies within regular parameters. Since many botnets use http as protocol to communicate with their C&C server, their communication would be hard to detect within networks with a high percentage of regular web traffic. Furthermore, any changing behavior within the network, for example caused by new software or even software updates, may cause the A-NIDS to generate an alarm. The false alarm rate of this type of detection technique is therefore rather high compared to other approaches. Beyond that, the analysis of the entire network communication may also be subject to legal restrictions.

Both kinds of NIDS still suffer from a limited scalability in order to handle large amount of traffic. To address this shortcoming, a technique called *netflow* is used to analyze less detailed connection information. Therefore, netflow is directly applied to routing devices in order to generate flow related information like source and destination IP-addresses, port numbers or protocol information. The payload of individual packets is not taken into account, which enables netflow to process larger amounts of traffic. The generated information is then forwarded to an analysis system that tries to detect malicious behavior. To reduce the load of the analysis system even further, incoming flow records can be sampled to process just a fraction of all records available. Even though netflow data misses valuable information contained in network connections, it is still possible to detect certain botnet characteristics by using netflow information only. One example for botnet behavior that can be detected by analyzing netflow data is so-called port scanning. Port scanning is used by infected systems to actively discover available services on remote machines by sending connection requests to various port numbers. If the according service is not available, the probed system will reject the incoming connection. While scanning a multitude of machines, a lot of rejected connections may occur within a network, which can be detected by analyzing netflow records. Another example is the distribution of spam emails. If a bot is used for sending out spam emails, it will create a lot of connections to a mail server, typically on port 25. These connections can be detected by analyzing netflow records and thus, the bot infection can be detected. On the other hand, the improved runtime performance comes at a price. Due to the exclusion of packet payloads, many other botnet activities can no longer be detected.

4.1.4 Honeypots

Most detection techniques face the major challenge of separating benign and botnet related activities apart. Honeypots on the other hand represent a vulnerable target that is used to trap attackers by providing various vulnerable services on purpose. If the honeypot is attacked, various kinds of information can be gathered about the attack and reported to the operator. Since honeypots do not serve for any other purpose, no regular user should ever interact with a honeypot. Overall, the only purpose of a honeypot system is getting attacked by infected machines and hence every interaction can be considered to be malicious.

Therefore, honeypots do not have to differentiate between benign and malicious activities, since every observed activity is inherently malicious. As this kind of honeypot acts like a server waiting for incoming connections from infected machines, it is also referred to as server honeypot. A direct consequence of this approach is a very low amount of false alarms and thus a reduced amount of information in total. Another major benefit of honeypots is that they are able to detect previously unknown botnets. Since honeypots do not use particular signatures or other previously known attack pattern in order to detect an attack, new attacks on the provided vulnerabilities can be detected. If the attack is successful, the attacking system will download a sample of its own botnet onto the honeypot in order to infect the system. As a result, honeypots are not only able to detect the attack in the first place but also to capture a copy of the attacking bot. This is still possible if the communication is encrypted since honeypots represent regular communication endpoints, which are able to decrypt incoming data streams.

Beside these benefits, honeypots may pose an additional threat to other systems in range. If a bot is able to completely infect a honeypot and start operating, the honeypot can be used to infect further systems. Another fundamental drawback is that attacks can only be detected by honeypots if they are attacked directly. If only other systems are attacked by a botnet, the attack remains undetected. To increase the probability to identify spreading botnets within an observed network, honeypots typically use a broad range of IP addresses. Another disadvantage of server honeypots is that they are only able to detect botnets that try to infect remote systems directly over the network. Botnets using other kinds of attack vectors, like malicious documents or websites, cannot by detected with this approach. Therefore, so-called client honeypots emulate vulnerable client applications, like web browsers or document viewers, in order to analyze suspicious files. Client honeypots may therefore browse the web or read spam emails like a regular user and open the received content. When suspicious documents are analyzed, client honeypots use signatures or dynamic heuristics to decide whether the analyzed content is malicious or benign. If the attack is used to download and install a bot sample, client honeypots are also able to capture a sample of the according bot.

Simulating client applications and analyzing suspicious documents as it is done by client honeypots is a rather different approach as it is used by server honeypots. While server honeypots can consider every interaction as malicious by definition, client honeypots have to separate malicious and benign documents apart. Beyond that, client honeypots cannot just wait for being attacked but have to actively search for potential malicious content. This results in an increased computational effort and also less precise results. Furthermore, client honeypots are more likely to generate false alarms than classic honeypots. This is caused since attacks are detected by heuristics during or after runtime. Thus, the malicious document can probe the runtime environment, or in this case the client honeypot, before the actual attack is launched. If the client honeypot can be exposed, the attack is aborted and the analyzed content behaves benign.

Active as well as passive honeypots can allow interactions as caused by an attacking botnet to a certain degree. Honeypots with a high degree of interaction, so-called high interaction honeypots, feature a full-blown operating to interfere with. Therefore, high interaction honeypots can be described as regular computer systems enhanced with various logging and analysis functionalities. As a result, high interaction honeypots are infected by an attack as any other regular system. A major benefit of this approach is that a lot of detailed information can be gathered on the attack and the according bot sample if this kind of honeypot gets infected. Every step from the initial attack to the completely infected system can be observed and analyzed. Beyond that, the behavior of the infected system can be observed as well. On the other hand, high interaction honeypots can pose a threat to other computer systems, since they can be used by botnets like any regular system. Furthermore, high interaction honeypots have to be reset after every successful infection attempt in order to provide exclusive information on newly registered attacks. Using a complete operating system and real vulnerabilities also results in a rather static configuration. High interaction honeypots are only able to generate information on attacks targeting a specific version or patch-level of the provided software and according vulnerabilities.

To overcome these shortcomings, so-called low interaction honeypots provide attacking botnets with a set of simulated vulnerabilities. Since the vulnerabilities are simulated, it is not possible for attacking botnets to gain access to the operating system and therefore the low interaction honeypot does not get infected. Instead, internal logic is used to automatically extract information from incoming requests, like commands used for downloading the bot sample. If this information can be successfully extracted, low interaction honeypots are also able to automatically download a copy of the attacking bot. As a result, low interaction honeypots do not have to be reset after every successful attack which makes them much more efficient. Since the bot is not executed on this kind of honeypot, it does not pose a severe threat to other computer systems in range. The simulation of vulnerabilities also brings more flexibility, since it is possible to simulate almost arbitrary vulnerabilities. Thus, it is possible to simulate vulnerabilities of different software versions or operating systems. It is even possible to dynamically simulate vulnerabilities depending on the initial request. If a request can be recognized as a request for a certain version or patch level, the according response can be returned. On the other hand, it might not always be possible to completely simulate certain attacks due to limited simulation capabilities. Low interaction honeypots also provide less information about the attacking bot, since it is not executed. Consequentially, the installation process as well as the runtime behavior of the bot is not observed.

Connecting various high interaction honeypots to a so-called honeynet can provide even more information on attacking botnets. Since the high interaction honeypots can be infected like regular systems, it is possible to observe the behavior of infected machines within a highly controlled environment. In this setup, it is for example possible to observe the spreading behavior or certain attacks launched by infected systems.

4.1.5 Spam-Traps

Another approach of detecting previously unknown botnets focuses on their malicious activity. One of the most prominent examples for malicious activities as carried out by botnets is the distribution of spam-emails. Therefore, bots are typically provided with a spam-template and a list of recipients. These spam-templates include the content of the spam-mail itself as well as a list of instruction on how certain parts of the content can be altered in order to prevent a signature based detection. The list of recipients on the other hand is a list of email addresses, which are commonly extracted from arbitrary websites. Therefore, specialized web crawlers, so-called harvesters, actively search the web and automatically extract containing email-addresses.

This process can be exploited in order to detect active botnets by creating dedicated email addresses, so-called spam-traps. Spam-traps are specially crafted email addresses that are placed on websites in order to be found by harvesters and thus to be used by spamming botnets. To ensure that spam-traps are used

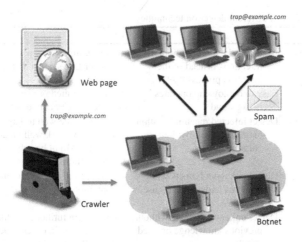

Fig. 4 Spam sent to harvested addresses by a botnet

by botnets only, they are usually hidden from regular users. This can be done by applying simple techniques like using white text on a white background or covering the spam-traps with other content. Harvesters on the other hand usually do not analyze if email addresses are actually visible and will thus use the spam-trap for spamming. The general principle of spam-traps is depicted in Fig. 4.

Received spam-emails can be used to detect even previously unknown botnets since they offer a lot of information. First of all, emails contain various header fields that are added by every mail server involved. Every mail server receiving or forwarding the spam mail will add the IP address of the system, from which the mail has been delivered. As a result, it is possible to trace received spam email back to the infected host that sent out the email in the first place. Besides detecting infected machines, spam emails can offer valuable additional information. In various cases, a copy of the attacking bot is directly attached to spam emails in order to infect receiving host systems by applying social engineering techniques. In other cases, the spam email might contain a link to an infected website which is used to infect victim systems. These links can be analyzed, for example by client honeypots, to receive a copy of the according botnet.

With the help of spam-traps, it is even possible to detect the harvester that is used by botnets to collect email addresses. Therefore, spam-trap email addresses on websites are generated dynamically depending on the IP address of the visiting system. If this email address is used for spamming afterwards, the IP address associated with the spam-traps email address belongs to the botnets harvester. A major drawback of spam-traps is that they are only able to detect botnets that are used for spamming. Detailed information about the causing botnet can only be gathered directly, if a copy of an according bot is attached to the spam-mails (Table 1).

In this section, various techniques to detect even previously unknown botnets have been presented. Each of the presented approaches uses different botnet characteristics for detection and has its own advantages and disadvantages. Therefore,

Table 1 Overview of different detection techniques

Technique	Pros	Cons
Log file analysis	Analyzes the effect of botnet infections instead of the infection process itself	Can be tampered by active bots on the according system. Huge amount of data
Antivirus	Easy to deploy and operates in background	Provides limited protection and can be deceived by active bots
Network analysis	Detect infected machines within entire networks by their communication	Does not scale well to large networks. May not work well on encrypted traffic. Might be subject to legal restrictions
Honeypots	Detect unknown botnets without previous knowledge on used attack	Are able to detect direct infection attempts only
Spam traps	Detect unknown botnets without previous knowledge on used attack	May require further tools like client Honeypots in order to detect the actual bot. Restricted to spam botnets

each technique is only able to detect a certain type of botnets sharing common characteristics like the same spreading technique or malicious activity. Thus, it is necessary to apply various techniques to detect arbitrary out-in-the-wild botnets to apply further countermeasures.

4.2 Analyzing

After having a botnet detected, the next step is analyzing the botnet to gain insight into the functioning of the botnet. This information is necessary for example to estimate the threat that is posed by an individual botnet, derive signatures for detection in antivirus solutions or to detect how bots can be removed from infected systems. Beyond that, detailed information on particular botnets may be used to develop individual countermeasures to actively combat the botnet's operation or to remotely disinfect according systems. Since bot samples are commonly available in binary form only, they have to be analyzed in order to reconstruct and understand their functionality. This process is also referred to as reverse engineering. The used techniques can be divided into dynamic analysis techniques, which analyze the bot during execution, and static analysis techniques that are used to analyze the content of a bot sample without execution. Both groups of techniques have their individual pros and cons and are both widely used to analyze current botnets. Therefore, the general concepts and technologies of both groups are introduced in the following section.

4.2.1 Dynamic Analysis

Dynamic analysis is used to observe the behavior of a particular bot sample during runtime. By executing a bot sample in an observed environment, it is possible to gather extensive valuable information. First information can be gathered immediately after the first execution by observing system state changes like created or modified files, created registry keys or spawned processes. This can be done either by tracking every modification on the analysis system or by comparing the system state before, during and after the execution. The gathered information contains details for example on how a bot infects a system and how it tries to ensure that it is reloaded after a system reboot. This information can be used immediately to derive disinfection routines in order to completely remove a bot from an infected system.

Observing the runtime behavior of a bot in general and its network communication in particular can also gather detailed information on the C&C infrastructure, spreading behavior and malicious activity. Like on every regular system, the running bot instance inside of the controlled environment will eventually contact its C&C server to receive new orders. The first information that can be gathered in this case is how the C&C server is addressed. It can be observed for example, if the bot directly connects to a hard coded IP address or if it tries to resolve one or more domain names. If the following communication is not encrypted, the communication between the bot and the C&C component can be further analyzed. Thus, it can be detected which protocol is used to communicate with the C&C component, e.g. IRC or HTTP, how the bot authenticates itself to the C&C component or what type of commands is sent back to the bot. If the bot receives the command to infect further systems, the propagation method can be also observed. It can be detected for example which services are attacked or how vulnerable systems are detected. If the bot receives commands to perform malicious activities like sending out spam emails or take part in distributed denial of service attacks, they can be further analyzed by observing the network communication.

One option to observe the runtime behavior of a malicious binary is by executing it within a debugger. Debuggers allow executing the bots' binary code step-by-step, which makes it easier for human analysts to understand the underlying logic. Furthermore, debuggers commonly allow modifying the examined binary, for example to disable anti-analysis routines. It is also possible to modify the values of internal variables, to trace different control flow paths and simulate certain events or inputs. Using debuggers to analyze a bot sample can therefore be used to gather detailed information on its functionality but still requires extensive human interaction. To complicate the analysis of bot samples by human analysts, they may be obfuscated for example by complicating the control flow. This obfuscated binary code may differ considerably from code that is generated by compilers, especially if original code is replaced by elongated code that is semantically equivalent or code that contains an above-average amount of jump instructions. As a result, it harder for analysts to trace individual control flows and thus to understand their functionality. Furthermore, bots can utilize additional anti-debugging techniques to complicate the usage of debuggers directly.

The entire process of executing and analyzing the runtime behavior of malicious binaries can also be automated by using so-called sandboxes. Sandboxes are special security tools that are used inspect and limit access from running processes to critical resources like system files. This allows the execution of bot samples within a restricted environment without the executing system being infected. Nevertheless, it is possible to analyze requests to restricted resources for example by using emulated resources instead. Commercial sandboxes typically provide extensive logging and analysis functionality to get an insight into an individual bot. Since sandboxes commonly provide a rather generic setup to provide extensive information on examined bot samples, the generated information is not focused on crucial functionality of individual bots. Therefore, bots are able to generate an overwhelming amount of information by extensively calling particular functions that are observed by the sandbox.

Instead of using available sandbox-solutions, the execution of bot samples can also be automated by using customized virtual machines, equipped with individual analysis tools. In both cases, the bot is executed in an environment that slightly differs from regular native systems. Therefore, it is possible for a bot to probe its runtime environment in order to detect analysis environments or even particular analysis tools before the actual task is performed. If it is possible to detect an analysis system, the bot can behave different from its regular behavior to deceive an analyst. An easier approach to prevent an analysis in special environments is by using a timer. In this case, the bot sleeps for a particular amount of time before it starts its actual execution. This may not be effective in case of a human analyst manually executing the bot, but it is certainly effective in case of automated dynamic analysis. Since time is a critical factor in automatically analyzing large sets of bot samples, common sandboxes terminate running samples after a few minutes. If the bot has not done nothing but waiting, no valuable information can be extracted by using dynamic analysis.

The use of a sleep timer reveals a fundamentally drawback of using dynamic analysis. This technique can only be used to gather information on the bots behavior that is shown during the limited timeslot in which it is being analyzed. Other functionality that is only used on an according command or at a particular time cannot be analyzed at all. Therefore, dynamic analysis is only able to analyze a subset of a bot's functionality in most cases. Another drawback of dynamic analysis is that it may not be strictly according to the law. When executing malicious code, there is the danger to take part in malicious activities that are performed by the examined malware, like sending out spam emails or participating in DDoS attacks.

4.2.2 Static Analysis

To get an insight into the entire functionality of a particular bot sample, it is necessary to analyze its binary code. By performing a so-called static analysis, it is possible to reverse the functionality of arbitrary code sequences in order to analyze the bots functionality in total. First of all, looking into the botnets binary code can revel various constants that are used by the bot, like domain names, IP addresses, command names or even passwords. The header of a bot sample can also contain information on used interfaces that are for example offered by system libraries.

In order to get more detailed information about the bot sample, like the used algorithms and data structures, it is necessary to analyze the instructions and the control flow within the bots binary code. Therefore, disassemblers are used to transform the binary code into a human readable representation. Unlike high-level representations of programs functionality like the source code of modern program languages, the generated representation consists of mnemonics, which indicate individual processor instructions. This representation is then divided into functional basic blocks to reconstruct the bots functionality step-by-step. A basic block is a code sequence that is executed at a stretch, without changing the control flow. Analyzing the control flow between these basic blocks can then reveal the underlying logic of the bots algorithms. By analyzing the implementation of the used algorithms it may be even possible to detect security flaws that can be exploited to apply active countermeasures against running bot instances. Results from static analysis can further be used to improve the results of dynamic analysis and the other way round. If a bot uses cryptography to protect its communication, it is for example possible to reconstruct the encryption key and algorithm in order to decrypt the observed traffic. Furthermore, it is possible to reveal the bots entire malicious functionality and detailed information on how an individual bot joins the C&C infrastructure.

Since the bot is not executed during static analysis, it cannot apply active countermeasures to hinder or even prevent its analysis. This however does not imply that bots do not try to counteract static analysis at all. In contrast, botnet authors anticipate their bots being statically analyzed and try to complicate the analysis process in advance. This is done by applying various techniques to modify the bots source code in a way that it is harder to analyze while maintaining the original functionality. A simple example for those techniques is so-called junk code insertion, where arbitrary code is added to the bots binary code that does not change the behavior of the remaining code. More sophisticated examples of code obfuscation are encryption, packing or virtualization of the bots code. These techniques work on a similar principle by modifying the bots binary code in advance and adding a small piece of code that is able to undo the modifications during runtime. In case of virtualization, the entire code is translated into code that is able to run on the included virtual machine, which makes it hard to reconstruct the original code. Since the bots sample contains the information on how these modifications can be undone, reverse engineering is still possible but requires various additional steps. Another challenge in static analysis may appear if a bot heavily relies on external sources. A bot may for example load code sequences or plugins directly from a C&C server into memory. In this case, the according code is only available in memory during runtime, which makes it hard to statically analyze the functionality of the bots code (Table 2).

Analyzing a bot sample in order to understand its functionality is an important part in countering active botnets. Reverse engineering can gather information on the bots C&C infrastructure, the implemented functionality and even the used algorithms and data structures. Dynamic analysis can be used to automatically extract valuable information from an individual bot sample. This information is

Table 2 Overview of different analysis techniques

Technique	Pros	Cons
Dynamic analysis	Can provide valuable information easily and can be automated	Can be deceived by botnets, provide incomplete information, may not be strictly according to the law
Static analysis	Provides comprehensive information on particular botnets. No legal issues	Time-consuming, manual work by high-skilled professionals needed. May be severely limited in special cases

however limited to the behavior that is actually shown by the bot during analysis. Static analysis on the other hand can be used to analyze the entire functionality of a bot sample. However, since bot authors commonly apply various obfuscation techniques, pattern matching can no longer be applied in order to assign particular code sequences to certain functionalities. Therefore, statically analyzing the functionality of a bot sample commonly requires a high amount of manual work. The gathered information can be used to derive disinfection routines or even to apply active countermeasures in order to combat active botnets.

4.3 Tracking

After having a botnet detected in the first place, it is possible to get an insight into the botnet's operation. This includes observing the botnet's operation like the performed frauds, which can be used to get information that is more detailed on the botnet's background and its botmaster's intentions. Therefore, information gathered from reverse engineering individual bot samples can be used to track the C&C communication of the according botnet. This communication can be analyzed for example to find out what kind of systems were hit by distributed denial of service attacks or what type of spam is distributed. It can be further observed if bots are commanded to attack remote systems in order to increase the size of the botnet or if the amount of infected machines remains constant. This information can be directly used to apply countermeasures against ongoing botnet attacks. If a server experiences a DDoS attack, tracking can be used to figure out which botnet is responsible for the particular attack. It is then possible to apply further approaches, like disconnecting the C&C server from the Internet, in order to stop ongoing attacks. This may not necessarily have a lasting effect on the botnets operation in total, but might stop the attack since machines will receive no more attack commands for the time being.

Another important aspect of tracking a botnet's communication is that many bots evolve during their lifetime. When botmasters detect security flaws in their botnet, they usually update their botnet for example to prevent according countermeasures. This could for example be observed for the Conficker botnet that used MD-6 as part of its encryption protocol. Shortly after a flaw in MD-6 had been published, the Conficker botmasters pushed an update with a fixed implementation [52]. By observing the botnet communication, updates can be detected to keep track of the latest version of the operating botnet.

Botnet tracking can also be used to detect new botnets. Particular bots, so-called droppers, are just used to install additional malware on the infected machines. This is also a common approach for botnets providing pay-per-install, where malware is installed as a service. By tracking the botnets communication, these malware samples can be downloaded and analyzed. If a malware is distributed by droppers only, there is no other way to automatically detect this malware than by tracking a botnets communication.

4.3.1 Running Observed Bot

A rather simple approach on tracking a botnet's communication is by infecting a vulnerable system on purpose and observing its communication. Instead of analyzing a bot's functionality in detail, as with sandboxes for example, this approach only aims to observe a bot's communication in order to track its operations. For this purpose, sandboxes would generate a large computational and information overhead as well as an increased risk of a bot behaving different from its normal behavior on regular systems. This approach can always be applied, but it usually comes with various disadvantages. Intentionally running a bot on a regular system does not only include the C&C communication but also malicious activities. Therefore, the observed bot can take part in its botnet's attacks just like any regular bot. This would also mean to consciously take part in cyber crime, which is illegal in most countries.

This approach also implies that the botnet's communication is somehow understandable, i.e., the communication is not encrypted. Otherwise, observing the communication of a bot is still possible but it requires more effort. In this case, the decryption algorithm has to be analyzed first by using reverse engineering, in order to create an according decryption routine. This also applies if the bot uses rather cryptic commands that cannot be associated directly with particular actions. Therefore, reverse engineering is also necessary to find out which action is associated with which command.

A general weakness of this approach is the limited scalability in order to track a higher amount of botnets. Since not every bot can run side-by-side with any other bot, every bot should run on its own physical system to avoid unpredictable side effects. Tracking thousands of different botnets, as it is done by various organizations, would hardly be possible by using this approach. It is also possible to run bots within a virtualized environment, but this may increase the risk of the bots behaving different than within native environments. Nevertheless, these approaches are still applicable to get a quick look into the communication of a particular botnet.

4.3.2 Specialized Tracking Tools

To observe larger amounts of botnets, specialized tracking tools are necessary that can be using to observe various botnets simultaneously. These tools only emulate the

Table 3 Overview of different techniques used for botnet tracking

Tracking technique	Pros	Cons
Running observed bot	Easy to apply, may be hard to detect from botmasters	Legal issues, does not scale well
Specialized tracking tools	Observe multiple botnets simultaneously	May require extensive preparation, risk of being detected by botmasters

communication part of an individual bot to mimic its behavior while joining the bot-nets C&C communication. Since the rest of the bot is not emulated, especially the malicious activity, those approaches are more compatible with applicable law. On the other hand, this approach requires a lot more information on the observed botnet than the execution and observation of a regular bot. In order to emulate a bot's communication, the used protocol has to be analyzed as far as possible. The emulated communication component has to be able to interpret every incoming command sent from the C&C infrastructure and send out the correct answer in response. If the protocol is only partially emulated, it is possible that the emulated communication is not able to correctly answer particular commands, which can be detected by the according botmasters. As a result, the emulated communication component may face countermeasures from the botmaster's side, for example in form of DDoS attacks. Existing tools to track botnets therefore provide some kind of proxy support to masquerade the system's IP address behind the proxies address. If the botmaster manages to detect the snooping system and starts to attack its address with a DDoS attack, the proxy can be changed to continue other ongoing observations.

Applying specialized tracking tools is commonly done to track either HTTP or IRC based C&C communication. Even though, specialized tracking tools can also be applied to observe the communication of peer-to-peer botnets in various cases (Table 3).

Tracking botnets is important to get a detailed insight into a botnet's operation. It can expose information on the intention of the according botmasters or even hints on the botmasters itself. The communication of a botnet can be tracked easily if the bot does not apply any sophisticated encryption schemes. Although the observation of an infected machine is always possible, it may require a lot of preparation and is most often subjected to legal restrictions. To be able to observe a multitude of bot-nets simultaneously, specialized tracking tools are used. These tools require at least an equivalent amount of preparation than observing a regular bot but do not take part in botnet driven attacks. Furthermore, these systems commonly apply extensive logging capabilities and proxy support to evade potential DDoS attacks.

4.4 Measuring

After heaving a new botnet detected, it is possible to get more information on its distribution or on the amount of infected machines. Therefore, analysis results can be used to remotely detect infected machines of a particular botnet.

This approach is especially useful for example to detect infected systems within an observed network or to get a general overview on the botnets' distribution. Depending on the used C&C protocol, there are different approaches on how to remotely expose infected systems, which are described in the following section. Measuring approaches commonly try to identify infected machines taking part in the C&C communication by their IP address. Therefore, these approaches are commonly not able to determine the actual amount of infected machines directly, especially when detecting and counting infecting machines on the Internet, but generate a more or less exact estimation on the total amount. This effect can occur for example if infected machines use dial-up connections to connect to the Internet, which get a new IP address assigned each time they connect. On the other hand, it is commonly only possible to detect machines that are connected to the C&C infrastructure while measuring, which inherently requires them to be running and online. Therefore, the measuring period should be sufficiently large in order to detect as much infected machines as possible, but also as short as possible to reduce the effect of single infected machines being detected with multiple IP addresses. When measuring infected systems of a peer-to-peer botnet, it may be possible that individual peers contain information about peers that are currently offline. Even though, it may still be hard to determine if these peers for example use dial-up Internet connections and are also known by other IP addresses.

In [53], a unique identifier has been detected within the communication of the Torpig botnet, allowing the authors to compare the actual amount of systems with the amount of unique IP addresses. After measuring the botnet for 1 h, the total amount of unique Bot identifiers below the total amount of unique IP addresses. In contrast after measuring both values for 1 day, the actual amount of detected machines was 36.5 % below the amount of unique IP addresses. Thus, given a number of bots in a botnet it is important to question the methods used to gain these numbers and be aware that this number might be just a very rough estimation of the real numbers of bot.

4.4.1 Sinkholing

A major challenge in observing infected machines taking part in a botnet's C&C communication is to measure their communication in the first place. In general, it is not possible to observe the communication of all infected machines at once, but only the communication of individual infected machines. The communication from these machines in turn does generally not provide any valuable information on other infected machines. Another approach would be to observe the communication of the C&C server, since all infected machines will connect to this server eventually. Unfortunately, this approach is commonly not available since the C&C server is usually beyond the control of botnet countering organizations.

To be still able to observe the communication of infected machines trying to contact their C&C server, their communication can be redirected or sinkholed. In this scenario, connection requests from infected machines are redirected to a dedicated sinkhole server. By evaluating incoming connection requests, infected machines can be exposed by their IP address. As a result, one can get an impression on the amount of systems trying to establish a connection. The implementation of this approach however requires the ability to redirect connection requests to the C&C server on infected machines simultaneously from remote.

The C&C communication of a particular botnet can be redirected for example, if the infected machines rely on the domain name system in order to address their C&C server (Fig. 5). This is called DNS-based sinkholing in the following. This approach can be directly applied within controlled networks if the according bots use a fixed domain name, for example in combination with fast fluxing, to determine the IP address of their C&C server. Since DNS requests are directed to the local name server by default, the local name server can be configured to respond to those requests with the IP address of the sinkhole server. Thus, all infected machines within this network trying to resolve their C&C server's domain name will be redirected to the sinkhole server. As a result, infected machines can be directly identified by their IP address.

Whereas this approach is limited to controlled networks, sinkholing can also be applied to redirect the C&C communication of a particular botnet within the entire Internet. This can be done for example, if a botnet uses domain fluxing to address its C&C server. Therefore, each bot calculates an identical set of domain names, for example with respect to the current date. These domain names are then resolved in order to determine the IP address of the C&C server. If a domain name cannot be resolved, the bots just continue with the next domain name or retry another day. This implies, that the actual C&C does not need to be available all the time, but only if new orders should be placed. Therefore, the botmasters also do not need to register all of the calculated domain names in advance, but only a selected subset. Conversely, other domain names that are not used

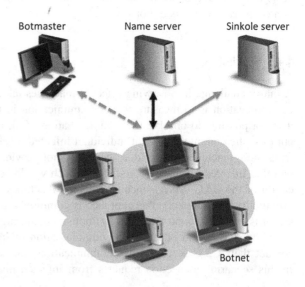

Fig. 5 Sinkholing C&C communication of a botnet based on DNS

by the botmasters remain freely available. By analyzing samples of a particular botnet, for example by applying reverse engineering techniques, it is possible to reconstruct the algorithm that is used to generate the domain names of the C&C server. As a result, it is possible to predict domain names that will be queried by the infected machines. Since the registration of domain names usually comes at a price, botmasters tend not to register all domain names in advance. By registering one of the predicted domain names for a sinkhole server, the communication of bots worldwide can be redirected. Thus, it is possible to determine the IP addresses of the infected machines and get an insight into the botnet's distribution.

DNS-based sinkholing is just one example on how the communication of an entire botnet can be redirected to almost arbitrary systems. A very similar approach can be applied in peer-to-peer based botnets, which is called Sybil-attack. In peer-to-peer based botnets, every bot knows about a relatively small subset of other bots, which are considered close with respect to a certain metric. By using this metric, messages within the peer-to-peer network are forwarded from one system to another, which is known to be closer to the intended destination. This routing technique can be exploited by deploying a large amount of fake peers distributed over the entire peer-to-peer address space. Thus, these fake nodes are likely to be known by a broad range of real bots and therefore to be part of the routing of C&C messages. Whenever a fake node receives a C&C message, it can be directly forwarded to a sinkhole server in order to identify infected machines. This approach has been successfully applied for example by [33] to sinkhole the communication of the Storm botnet. A less invasive approach as followed by [54] is just to forward incoming C&C messages like a normal bot participating in the peer-to-peer network. By storing the sender addresses of the forwarded C&C messages, participating bots can also be identified.

4.4.2 Peer-To-Peer Enumeration

Peer-to-peer can also offer further opportunities to actively identify infected machines. When a new bot joins the peer-to-peer network, it needs to know about a certain amount of other infected machines in order to take part in the routing of C&C messages. The process of a peer joining a peer-to-peer network is called bootstrapping, where other peers are informed about the new peer and information about other existing peers is gathered. A common way to achieve this is by using a small set of initial peers, for example hard coded within a bot's binary code, and querying these systems for further systems. This step can be repeated with returned bot addresses, for example until a certain amount of known peers is reached.

This bootstrapping process can be exploited to actively enumerate a botnet's peer-to-peer network in order to identify all participating peers. Therefore, reverse engineering techniques may be applied to reconstruct the bootstrapping protocol of a particular botnet. With this Information, existing peers can be queried for other known peers as it is done by a regular bot joining the network. The returned peers can then again be queried for further known peers until every reachable peer has been discovered. If the peer-to-peer network is fragmented into various sets of nodes that are not connected with each other, only systems within one connected set can be detected. Furthermore, systems that cannot be reached directly from the Internet, like machines behind a NAT router, cannot be queried at all. It is also not guaranteed that these machines are returned from other peers, since the receiver may not connect to these machines anyway. Therefore, actively enumerating a peer-to-peer network may only result in infected machines that can be reached directly over the Internet. This approach may also require a certain amount of time and it may not be easy to decide, when all available peers are discovered. Since other peers can constantly join or leave the network and rejoin with new IP addresses, it can be hard to decide which nodes have already been discovered. However, this approach can be successfully applied in various cases like [55], where the peer-to-peer botnet Nugache has been enumerated.

4.4.3 Fast-Flux Polling

Botnets that rely on Fast-Flux-Services in order to address their command and control server can also be actively enumerated. This kind of botnets use a fixed set of domain names that refer to a constantly changing set of proxy nodes. Bots that try to connect to their C&C server resolve these domain names and contact one of the resolved proxy nodes. These proxy nodes then forward the communication of the infected machines to the actual C&C server.

If the used domain names can be determined, for example by applying dynamic analysis techniques like sandboxing, it is possible to constantly resolve these domain names in order to determine new proxy nodes. This so-called fast-flux polling can therefore be used to determine a valuable set of infected machines. On the other hand, it is not guaranteed that discovered proxy nodes are part of the examined botnet at all. The botnet may just have rented a fast-flux service from another botnet and therefore, only infected machines of the other botnet can be determined. Even if all proxy nodes belong to the intended botnet, the fraction of infected machines that act as proxy nodes can be rather low. Since just infected machines that are directly reachable from the Internet can act as proxy nodes, the fraction of machines that can be detected by fast-flux polling is rather low. Furthermore, there is no guarantee that all directly reachable systems are used as proxy nodes at all. As with other approaches, it can be also hard to decide if resolved systems have already been detected before, due to potential dynamic IP addresses (Table 4).

Various techniques can be applied to measure the amount of infected systems and the distribution of particular botnets. Each approach can be used for different C&C architectures and is able to detect a different fraction of infected machines. Most approaches are only able to detect infected systems that are currently running and connected to the Internet. In contrast, peer-to-peer enumeration approaches may also result in IP addresses of peers that are currently offline. Due to the dynamic of IP addresses, these measuring results can differ from the

Table 4 Overview of different measurement techniques

Technique	Pros	Cons
Sinkholing	Can detect all infected and active systems worldwide	May require extensive preparation. May be rather expensive
Peer-to-peer enumeration	Can be hardly prevented by botmasters	May not be able to detect all active systems, may require extensive preparation
Fast-flux polling	Easy to apply, only little preparation needed	May provide rather limited information only

actual amount of infected machines. Therefore, measuring results should be interpreted with care since the raw numbers as generated by DNS based sinkholing may tend to overestimate the size of examined botnets. Active enumeration results like fast-flux polling on the other hand may only detect a small fraction of all infected machines. Consequently, measuring techniques can be inaccurate to gather a detailed insight into a botnets distribution worldwide. On the other hand, DNS based sinkholing can be reliably applied to determine infected systems for example within control networks like business networks.

5 Fighting Botnets

Gathered information on active botnets can be used to apply various countermeasures in order to restrict or even stop their ongoing operations. Mitigating the damage caused by active botnets however is only one step in fighting botnets in a durable and sustainable manner. Additionally to fighting the symptoms of today's cyber crime by shutting down existing botnets, it is also important to address the root cause that leads to the development of more and more sophisticated and dangerous botnets. Taking down individual botnets has only little sustainable impact on the global threat by itself, since other botnets will fill the gap eventually. Instead, it is also important to prevent new infections and beyond that, combat the underlying business model of today's botnets.

The following section deals with various techniques to fight the botnet threat on these different levels. First of all, different approaches are discussed to prevent further systems from getting infected by botnets. Techniques to combat existing botnets are described subsequently. This is followed by various techniques that can be applied in order to minimize the profit generated by botnets. Combating botnets on these levels addresses the threat as it is caused by currently operating botnets on the one hand, and the causes that lead to constant new botnets on the other.

5.1 Prevent New Infections

Current botnets do not need to apply sophisticated attacks in order to infect new systems in many cases. Recent reports show that 41 % of surveyed end users do not use up-to-date security software [56]. In other cases, users do not install security updates regularly, allowing botnets to successfully exploit already known vulnerabilities. But even if computer systems are fully patched and equipped with latest security software, they are still threatened severely by social engineering attacks. Instead of developing new and complicated attack techniques, malware authors heavily rely on the help of end users in order to infect their systems.

A consequence of this situation is that botnets commonly find a lot of vulnerable systems to infect, which makes botnets particularly interesting for cyber criminals. Another consequence is that the development of new botnets is rather cheap. Parts of already existing botnets can be largely reused, which dramatically reduces the development effort. The use of social engineering instead of using complex exploits also reduces the effort needed to develop and deploy new botnets. Therefore, it is rather cheap for cyber criminals to distribute new botnets, which are then used for example to generate revenue. Increasing computer security on the other hand, by applying state-of-the-art security software and awareness against social engineering techniques, would also make it more difficult for cyber criminals to create new botnets. Even if it might be impossible to prevent infections with absolute certainty, the development effort for cyber criminals might no longer be covered by generated revenue. Furthermore, improved host security would also slow down the distribution of already active botnets. In combination with the disinfection of infected machines, this provides a sustainable way in combating existing botnets.

The following section describes different approaches on preventing new infections on a technical as well as on a user level. Technical prevention techniques are deployed on host systems in order to prevent exploits from being successful and therefore preventing the system from being infected. User level countermeasures on the other hand address the behavior of end users in order to prevent social engineering attacks.

5.1.1 System Hardening

Even though various modern botnets use highly sophisticated infection techniques and 0-day exploits, from which systems can hardly be protected, many other infections could be prevented. During the first half of 2011, only 0.12 % of all registered attacks were caused by 0-days [51]. In contrast, the vast majority of registered exploits target vulnerabilities that might have already been closed by security updates several months ago. As a consequence, all infections caused by these attacks may have been prevented by the installation of already available security updates. Installing security updates as soon as possible is therefore one important step to prevent new botnet infections.

In other cases, security updates may not be available within short time periods. Various vulnerabilities may even remain unpatched for years [57], leaving systems using the according software open to botnet attacks. To detect and mitigate attacks targeting known vulnerabilities, antivirus solutions can be used. By applying signature based detection techniques, dynamic heuristics and sandboxing of suspicious files, antivirus solutions are able to detect even unknown botnet samples. Antivirus solutions cannot, however, provide full protection with absolute certainty. By applying various obfuscation techniques, malware authors try to prevent a signature-based detection by antivirus solutions. Due to the large amount of newly detected obfuscated malware samples per day [58], it is no longer possible to reliably detect samples of even known malware by signature-based detection techniques. In other cases, antivirus solutions may whitelist digitally signed files with trusted signatures [59]. Malware signed with stolen certificates like Stuxnet is therefore able to pass security checks without problems. Finally, antivirus solutions have to cope with a fundamental challenge, since they have to operate on potentially infected systems. Therefore, running malware on infected systems may actively prevent its detection by applying rootkit technology in order to hide malicious files from antivirus solutions. In other cases, malware just disables any present antivirus software right after a successful infection. As a result, antivirus solutions are not able to reliably protect vulnerable host systems from infections by current malware or botnets. Nevertheless, antivirus solutions provide additional security to host systems and should therefore also be used as part of a basic protection in order to prevent new botnet infections.

Another important part in preventing new infections is reducing the amount of potential vulnerabilities. Since software possibly contains exploitable vulnerabilities, reducing the amount of software can help to prevent new infections. This especially applies for running services that are not essentially needed in regular daily operations. By disabling these unneeded services, the overall security of an individual host system can be improved, without affecting the needed operational capabilities. Another way to prevent existing services from being attacked from the Internet is by applying firewalls with according filter rules. By using firewalls, incoming connections to existing services can be blocked, without having to actually uninstall or disable the entire service. Using firewalls also provides more flexibility, for example by enabling certain services for selected remote systems only. Thus, by applying appropriate filter rules, potential vulnerable services can be used by individual trusted systems only, reducing the risk of an infection. Consequentially, disabling unnecessary services and restricting existing services to particular remote systems can also help in preventing new botnet infections.

5.1.2 Awareness

Beside technical countermeasures trying to prevent infection attempts from being successful, another major component in preventing new infections is addressing the user behavior. In fact, many end users are not completely aware of the threat that is posed by email attachments or other content from the Internet. In addition, cyber criminals use more and more sophisticated social engineering techniques in order to trick end users into opening malicious files from the Internet.

One way to infect new systems by exploiting inappropriate user behavior is by tricking users into manually downloading and executing a copy of a bot without using any software vulnerabilities at all. Therefore, the malicious executable is commonly advertised as some form of useful utility application, for example needed to display postcards or video files. If the malicious executable also contains the previously advertised functionality, most users won't even become suspicious while their system is being infected in background. In order to get users into manually downloading the malicious file, users are commonly directed to according web pages with the help of e.g., spam emails, social networks or twitter. If a bot for example manages to capture the address book on infected machines, it is even possible to create spam messages for individual recipients with known sender addresses or social network as well as twitter accounts.

Another commonly used technique used to trick users into downloading malicious executable files is by imitating system windows within the browser. This technique is particularly used by so-called rouge AV software. Therefore, the window of common security software like the windows security center is displayed within a browser window, telling the user that his system is infected by a multitude of malware. To disinfect the system, a download link to pseudo antivirus software, the rouge AV software, is provided to the user. If the rouge AV software is installed on the user's system, it may act as any regular antivirus software in order to prevent the user from becoming suspicious. The software may even disinfect various infections, except the infection that is caused by the malware that is contained within the rouge AV software. Depending on the underlying business model, the user may even have to pay money for the rouge AV software or for the disinfection.

Besides tricking the user into installing the malware directly, another commonly used approach is to exploit vulnerabilities in client applications. Therefore, infected documents like PDF or office documents are used as well as infected web pages. If a user opens infected content with a vulnerable client application, like a PDF viewer or browser, the system can get infected automatically in background. These malicious documents are commonly distributed directly as attachment within spam emails. In other cases, the spam email may contain a link directing the user to a malicious web page that may directly infect the users system by exploiting vulnerabilities within the browser or browser plugins. Therefore, so-called exploit kits can be used to easily create malicious web Pages that are able to exploit various vulnerabilities in different browser versions or plugins.

A major advantage of using social engineering techniques in order to infect new systems is that malicious content is actively downloaded onto the victims system. Thus, corresponding attacks can be applied even if the victim's system is not directly reachable from the Internet. This is for example the case, if the victim's system is protected by a firewall or located within a local network behind a NAT router. As a result, recent studies have shown that almost half of analyzed attacks rely on user interaction in order to be successful [51]. By raising the awareness of the threat that is posed by various online content, for example by information campaigns, the amount of botnet infections relying on user interaction could be dramatically reduced.

In order to raise the awareness and support end users in securing or disinfecting their computer systems, various initiatives have already been founded. National initiatives like [60] offer free disinfection tools and provide information on the threat that is posed by botnets. Providing simple and straightforward instructions is crucial, since many users are still overstrained in securing or disinfecting their systems, even though they know about potential threats. Therefore, these kinds of initiatives can have an important contribution to prevent new botnet infections.

5.2 Mitigate Existing Botnets

Whereas the prevention of new infections slows down the spreading of currently active botnets, infected systems are not affected directly. As a result, by relying on the prevention of new infections only, already active botnets are still able to operate regularly. They are therefore still able to send out spam emails, launch DDoS attacks or steal data from infected machines. To cope with the threat that is posed by existing botnets, various additional approaches can be applied. These approaches can be divided into techniques mitigating the attacks launched by botnets on the one hand and techniques directly combating a botnet on the other. The latter can further be divided into techniques used to mitigate a botnets operation, for example by disrupting the C&C communication, or techniques aiming to disinfect according systems.

Approaches to mitigate existing botnets also provide different sustainability. Various techniques preventing individual botnet attacks or disrupting the C&C communication of a botnet only temporarily mitigate a botnet's operation. Since countermeasures usually come at a price, each countermeasure will be discontinued eventually. As a result, the botnet may not only be able to resume its regular operations, but is also warned about individual weaknesses. Therefore, the botmasters are able to modify their botnet in order to prevent individual countermeasures from being successful again.

Applying sustainable techniques on the other hand to permanently combat an existing botnet usually requires complex preparations and an invasive interaction with the according botnet. Since bots are running on illegally infected systems, applying these techniques also includes interacting with these systems. As even extensive testing of individual countermeasures cannot guarantee that no damage is caused to the affected systems, applying these techniques raises ethical and legal questions. Tikk et al. [61] for a further discussion on these questions.

The following section discusses various approaches that are used to technically mitigate existing botnets. As with other techniques, there is no general-purpose technique to combat existing botnets, but a set of different approaches targeting individual botnet characteristics. Furthermore, the presented approaches combat botnets on different levels and require different invasive interactions with infected machines. These approaches include techniques used to disrupt a botnets communication or even disinfect machines of a particular botnet.

5.2.1 Sinkholing

Sinkholing, as already described in Sect. 4.4.1, is used to redirect a botnet's communication to a particular server. This is commonly done by changing DNS records that are used by botnets to identify their C&C server, to point to a dedicated sinkhole server. This can be used for example, to identify infected machines trying to contact their C&C server, but sinkholing can also be applied as a countermeasure. If the entire communication of a botnet can be redirected from the actual C&C to a sinkhole server, no infected machine is able to receive new orders. Thus, the botnet cannot be commanded anymore by the botmaster and is therefore unable to act. Currently running attacks will expire eventually, at the latest when all participating systems have been restarted. There is, however, the risk, that individual botnets will continue their latest activity after rebooting the system. This case, the attack will continue until the systems have been disinfected.

Using sinkholing in order to prevent infected machines from contacting their actual C&C server however may require considerably more effort than just identifying infected machines. In case of domain-fluxing, infected machines will try to contact the C&C server by a set of pseudo randomly generated domain names. If the C&C server cannot be reached by one of the generated domain names, the next domain name is used. Successfully connecting to the actual C&C server requires the expected behavior of the requested server, in form of correct responses to connection request corresponding to the botnets C&C protocol. If the server does not correspond as expected, the bots will continue with the next domain name. Thus, infected machines can be identified by their connection attempt, but they are still able to contact their actual C&C server. Therefore, the botnet needs to be analyzed first to be able to emulate the connection establishment of a real C&C server. This can be done for example by observing a bot's communication with its C&C server or by applying other reverse engineering techniques. If the emulation of a C&C server's connection establishment succeeds, infected machines will get caught by the sinkhole server and thus no longer be able to contact their C&C server.

This countermeasure can also be applied to redirect the communication within P2P-based botnets. As already described in Sect. 4.4.1, it can be possible to the P2P network with various fake peers. These peers can then be used to redirect connections that are routed via fake peers to a sinkhole server. Using strategically optimized peer addresses or using a large number of fake peers increases the probability of fake peers involved in the routing of C&C messages. By using specialized tools and virtualization techniques, the necessary amount of physical resources can be largely reduced. This so-called Sybil-attack can be used to redirect connection requests to the C&C server to prevent infected machines from contacting their C&C server. Depending on the particular botnet, it may also be possible to just drop connection requests to the C&C server on fake peers.

Sinkholing a botnet's communication in order to prevent infected machines from contacting their C&C server can be applied without major ethical concerns, since no invasive interaction with infected machines is necessary. Sinkholing however may require a considerable effort to be successful. Furthermore, sinkholing the entire communication of a botnet may be rather cost intensive, for example if many domain names have to be registered. This can be exploited by botmasters by making it rather expensive to sinkhole the botnets communication. Conficker.C for example generates as many as 50,000 domain names each day. Sinkholing all domain names would cost between \$91.3 million and \$182.5 million per year according to [53]. Finally, the risk of individual infected machines continuing their malicious activities while their communication is sinkholed remains.

5.2.2 P2P-Polluting

To combat P2P-based botnets, a technique called P2P polluting can be applied. Within a P2P network, no peer knows about all other peers in general. Instead, every peer only maintains a list of active peers considered close with respect to a certain metric. Furthermore, individual peers commonly store a limited amount of other peers only. This can be exploited, by announcing a huge amount of fake peers to existing peers of a P2P-based botnet. In contrast to a Sybil-attack, these peers do not have to exist at all, since they are just used to fill up the peer lists of other peers. By infiltrating a large amount of fake peers to a bot's peer list, it can be possible to overwrite all entries of actual peers. Consequentially, the bot would no longer be able to communicate with any other bot and thus to reach its C&C server.

Applying this technique to individual bots however does not prevent these bots from being contacted by other bots. Since bots may exchange known peers, this may result in fake peers propagating to other bots. On the other hand, this may also result in real peers being announced to the manipulated peer by other peers. Consequentially, it is possible that a manipulated bot recovers connectivity to other bots and is thus again able to participate the P2P network regularly. To prevent the P2P network from recovering, it may be necessary to overwrite peer lists of all bots, to stop the entire P2P communication at once. Thus, no bot is able to contact any other bot and no message can be forwarded from one peer to another. Consequentially, no bot is able to contact its C&C server and cannot receive new orders.

P2P-polluting however requires certain characteristics of a P2P-based botnet to be successful. It has to be possible to add fake peers to other peers and thus overwrite known existing peers. A possible countermeasure would be to probe new peers before they are added to the peer list in order to prevent fake peers to be added. On the other hand, this technique requires only limited interaction with individual peers and thus raises little ethical and legal concerns.

5.2.3 C&C Server Takedown

A classic approach in countering existing botnets is to takedown their C&C server. If it is possible to identify the C&C server of a particular botnet, for example by applying reverse engineering techniques, this server can be shut down or disconnected from the Internet. Depending on applicable law, this might be done for example by according Internet service providers on behalf of law enforcement agencies. If the C&C server is no longer available, the botmasters are no longer able to send out new commands to their botnet. Thus, the botnet will not be able to perform new malicious activities but may continue already ongoing ones.

Taking down individual C&C servers requires only little preparation in analyzing the botnet. The actual execution of this countermeasure also requires little effort, compared with other countermeasures like sinkholing a botnets C&C communication. Since this is anticipated by botmasters, they commonly implement techniques allowing them to regain control over their botnet after a C&C server has been taken down. This is done for example by using domain-fluxing techniques, allowing the botmasters to add a new C&C server easily. Thus, the takedown of an individual C&C server may have no lasting impact on the according botnet.

5.2.4 Remote Disinfection

Whereas other approaches target the C&C server or communication, it may also be possible to disinfect infected machines of a botnet directly. In contrast to the former approaches, disinfecting infected machines from remote can be used to actually remove an existing botnet. Blocking a botnet's communication for example just sedates a botnet by preventing it from receiving new orders. Consequentially, the botnet itself is still present and thus still posing a threat. Even if the bots do not perform any malicious activities, they still may cause the infected system to run unstable or may contain security flaws allowing attacks to gain access to the system.

Security flaws of individual botnets may also provide the opportunity to disinfect infected systems from remote. Therefore, the network may be actively scanned for infected systems, for example based on services provided by infected machines. In other cases, regular services on infected machines may behave slightly different [34], what can also be used to identify infected machines from remote. According security flaws on infected machines can then be used to gain access to these systems in order to execute disinfection routines.

Another way to disinfect infected machines from remote is by using the C&C communication of a botnet. In various cases, botnets support an update command to replace the existing bot with a new or updated version [62]. By using reverse engineering to reconstruct the bots C&C protocol and the according parameters used for the update command, it can be possible to send a manually crafted update command to infected machines. This update command can be used to replace the bot on infected machines with something benign like a tool to remove all bot related files. In other cases, bots may even support an uninstall command, that can be directly used to disinfect according systems from remote. To send the commands to the infected machines, sinkholing techniques may be used to redirect the botnet's communication to a server sending out the according commands.

Disinfecting infected systems from remote may not necessarily mitigate an existing botnet permanently. Since the update- or remove-command will only disinfect remote systems that are joining the C&C communication while the commands are sent out, it is unlikely that all systems will get disinfected at once. Consequentially, the remaining infected systems may just reinfect the disinfected

Table 5 Overview of different techniques to mitigate existing botnets

Technique	Pros	Cons
Sinkholing	Can sedate entire botnets over extensive periods of time	Requires extensive preparation. May be rather expensive
P2P-polluting	Can sustainably disrupt the communication of P2P-based botnets	Requires extensive preparation and can be applied in particular cases only
C&C server takedown	Can be applied quickly without much preparation. Disrupts the entire C&C communication	May not have a lasting impact on the according botnet. C&C server has to be within area of responsibility
Remote disinfection	Removes the botnet instead of just disrupting its communication	May require extensive preparation, legal and ethical issues

systems. To have a lasting impact on the according botnet, it is therefore necessary to close the security flaw used by the botnet while disinfecting. As a result, the particular botnet can be eliminated almost completely, which also removes the threat posed to all systems involved.

Nevertheless, disinfecting infecting systems requires invasive interaction with all infected machines. Moreover, it cannot be guaranteed that the disinfection process can be performed without any complication, regardless of the amount of testing. It is also practically not possible to ask all system owners for permission, since they can be distributed across countries worldwide. As a result, disinfecting systems from remote involves gaining illegal access to remote systems, albeit with good intentions. Thus, applying this approach raises ethical and legal concerns, since the approach is quite similar to the infection process used by cyber criminals. Furthermore, it has to be clarified who is responsible for possible complications during the disinfection process (Table 5).

In the previous section, different techniques to combat existing botnets have been introduced. These techniques aim to disrupt a botnet's regular operation in order to incapacitate the botnet or to even disinfect according host systems. These techniques can be applied depending on the C&C architecture of the targeted botnet. Beyond these approaches it is possible in many cases to apply custom countermeasures in order to combat individual botnets. Even though it is possible to effectively counter existing botnets on a technical level, the according approaches cannot be applied in practice. Various approaches require invasive interaction with the targeted botnet, which implies an interaction with individual infected host systems. This raises ethical concerns and may risk the operation of affected host systems. Furthermore, there is no legal certainty, allowing particular countermeasures to be applied. Other approaches requiring less interaction with infected machines do not remove the botnet itself, leaving a residual risk to systems involved. Furthermore, applying technical countermeasures does not mitigate the global botnet threat, since it does not prevent new botnets from emerging. Therefore, these techniques have to be applied alongside with other approaches in order to reach a sustainable impact on today's threat landscape.

5.3 Minimizing Profit

Complicating the infection of new systems and combating active botnets may result in a temporary reduction of the botnet threat, but it will not end the arms race between cyber criminals on the one hand and countering parties on the other. As long as botnets can be used to generate revenue with a justifiable effort, organized crime will most likely continue to rely on botnets. Hardening individual host systems will result in even more sophisticated exploit or social engineering techniques to fill the gap as created for example by the takedown of individual botnets.

Since most botnets are used to generate revenue, fighting this threat requires minimizing the net profit that can be generated by botnets as far as possible. Therefore, it is necessary to increase the development and maintenance costs as well as to decrease the profitability of malicious activities. Techniques to prevent new infections, like hardening of individual host systems, will already increase the effort needed to infect new systems. Mitigating active botnets will further reduce the life cycle of a botnet, reducing the possible amount of malicious activities in consequence. To reduce the possible net profit of botnets even further, the impact of individual malicious activities can be mitigated in order to reduce their profitability. As a result of these approaches, it may no longer be profitable to develop and operate new botnets. In the following section, various techniques aiming to reduce the revenue, which can be generated by individual malicious activities, are discussed.

5.3.1 BGP Blackholing

BGP is a routing protocol applied within gateway routers between different autonomous systems (AS). An AS is a set of networks operated by a single institution that is administrated as a single entity. BGP therefore maintains a table about paths between different ASs identified by their IP prefixes. Thus, BGP is able to forward IP packets to the target AS, according to their prefix, where they can be transmitted to the according host. The involved routers usually have a special route to a so-called null interface, which drops all forwarded traffic.

This can be used to drop DDoS related traffic, in order to maintain the availability of the targeted host. This can be done by dropping all outgoing traffic from the AS containing the attacking hosts targeting the AS of the victim system. Alternatively it is possible to drop all incoming traffic from AS that contain attacking systems at the AS containing the target host. Both approaches can be used to effectively mitigate ongoing DDoS attacks while the approach is applied. As soon as the blackholing discontinues, the DDoS attack can proceed. Launching denial of service attacks is commonly offered by botnets as a service. Reducing the effect of DDoS attacks may cause costumers to lose interest in this kind of malicious service and thus reduce the revenue that is generated by the botnet.

The major disadvantage of this approach is that it generates a rather high degree of collateral damage. This is caused by the fact that not only DDoS related traffic is dropped, but also the entire benign traffic between attacking and victim AS. Thus, BGP blackholing can only be applied for short time periods in general. Furthermore, BGP blackholing is not suitable for DDoS attacks originated from infected systems distributed over various different AS.

5.3.2 Blacklisting

If certain resources are known to be malicious, blacklisting is used to prevent these resources from communicating with other resources. Although various kinds of blacklists exist, the underlying principle is always the same. If one resource is detected to be malicious, it is added to a central database. Other resources query this database before connecting to or accepting connections from a remote resource in order to check if the resource is known to be malicious. If the resource is contained within the blacklist database, the connection attempt is aborted or rejected.

A common example for the use of blacklists is blocking mail servers that are mainly used to distribute spam emails. If such a mail server can be detected, its domain name is added to a blacklist. If the blacklisted mail server tries to forward spam emails to a regular mail server, the regular mail server will look up the domain name of the sending mail server und thus reject the spam mails. Since this approach is widely used in practice, not yet blacklisted mail servers are outsold on the black market [63]. Nevertheless, blacklisting is used to effectively reduce the total amount of delivered spam emails and thus to combat botnet activities. Distributing spam emails is also commonly provided by botnets as a service. Reducing the amount of spam emails that can be sent by individual botnets also reduces the revenue that can be generated by offering this service.

Another common example of blacklisting is blocking web pages that are known to be malicious. Therefore, the URLs of these web pages are also added to a central database. Whenever a user tries to access a web page with its browser, the browser checks if the requested URL is blacklisted. If so, the user can be warned about the malicious website. Thus, blacklisting can also be used to mitigate new botnet infections via infected web pages.

A general drawback of blacklisting is that it may take some time until malicious resources are blacklisted. Until then, malicious resources are able to operate normally and send out spam email for example without restrictions. Blacklisting also provides a temporal mitigation of malicious botnet activities only. If a botnet switches to other resources like other mail servers, it can continue its malicious activity.

5.3.3 Port Blocking

Botnets commonly rely on unauthenticated services on port 25 to distribute spam emails. Common examples for these services are so-called open relay mail server, which are misconfigured mail servers that can be used without authentication. Legitimate mail services should use authentication instead, for example on port 587. If using unauthenticated mail services is almost dedicated to malicious activities, blocking port 25 can dramatically reduce the amount of distributed spam emails [64]. Consequentially, this would also reduce the revenue that can be generated by distributing spam emails.

A drawback of this approach is that it would also block any benign services using port 25. This is, however, less critical since benign services could switch to another port. Misconfigured mail servers that accept unauthenticated mails on port 25 would still be blocked efficiently, for example by involved ISPs.

5.3.4 Walled Garden

In various cases, ISPs are able to detect botnet infections on their costumer's systems. This can be done by evaluating netflow records in order to detect infected machines participating in DDoS attacks or sending out spam emails. Beyond that, other detection or measuring techniques like honeypots or spam traps can be applied by ISPs with respect to their customer's privacy in order to detect infected machines of individual botnets. If the infection of individual systems is detected, a technique called walled garden can be applied. Therefore, infected machines can be disconnected from the Internet. To support the disinfection of the according systems, all web requests can be redirected to a dedicated web page, providing information on how to disinfect the system. Furthermore, all web pages of malware mitigation services can be whitelisted in order to provide users of infected systems with all information and tools needed to disinfect their systems.

Applying walled gardens to infected computer systems can effectively reduce the profitability of individual botnets. Disconnecting infected systems performing malicious activities from the Internet directly reduces the extent of these activities. Infected machines are therefore for example able to send less spam, infect fewer systems or participate in DDoS attacks for a limited time only. Consequentially, applying walled gardens directly reduces the profitability of these activities. Assuming that every system will get connected back to the Internet after a successful disinfection only, each bot that has been detected is permanently lost for the botmaster. Furthermore, the risk of getting disconnected from the Internet may further increase the effort of individual users to protect their systems form malware.

To be able to apply walled gardens, infected system have to be detected reliably in order to prevent the accidental disconnection of uninfected systems. Furthermore, significant side effects may occur when disconnecting customers from the Internet, for example the connection is also used for telephony. Applying restrictive walled gardens may also not be accepted by various customers. Consequentially, ISPs may have limited interest in applying walled gardens since they may not be interested in loosing these customers. Furthermore, the legal situation for applying walled gardens is rather difficult in many countries.

5.3.5 Encryption of Valuable Information

A common malicious activity of botnets is to steal valuable information from infected machines, which is sold on the black market. Especially data extracted from corporate systems can generate high profits for botmasters. Individual sources like [65] describe corporate data already as the latest currency of cyber-crime. In the recent past botnets like GhostNet have been specially designed for this purpose [8].

To reduce the amount of valuable information that can be extracted from infected machines, this information can be encrypted. It should be noted, that encrypting the entire hard disk does not prevent botnets from stealing information, since all requested information is automatically decrypted just like for any regular user. Instead, valuable information can be encrypted separately and decrypted on demand only. Similar approaches can be applied on non-corporate host systems, for example by not storing login credentials on the systems. Consequentially, massively increasing the effort for botnets accessing valuable information on infected machines also reduces the revenue that can be generated by selling this information on the black market (Table 6).

Mitigating malicious activities performed by botnets can be used to efficiently reduce the revenue that can be generated. Since financial interests are the most common reason to operate botnets, reducing the potential revenue will also reduce the motivation to develop and operate new botnets. Therefore, various techniques that can be applied to reduce the impact of individual activities have been discussed. Alongside with other countermeasures increasing the development costs for botnets, this may result in botnets no longer being profitable. Consequentially, the threat posed by botnets can be mitigated in an effective and sustainable manner.

6 Botnets: The Way Ahead

The threat posed by current botnets affects almost all kinds of computer systems today. Despite all currently available countermeasures, this threat cannot be expected being eliminated in near future. Thus, it is even more important to learn the lessons from the past in order to be more effective to combat botnets prospectively. The evolution of botnets has resulted in highly organized criminal organizations within a comprehensive underground economy. Botnets are professionally developed and commercially distributed. These botnets are kept up-to-date and use cutting edge technology to serve their malicious purpose. This development can be expected to continue, which requires major efforts from countering organizations. The applied countermeasures were commonly applied as a reaction on individual observed botnets, leaving the edge to cyber criminals. Anticipating the future development of botnet technologies can therefore help to apply particular countermeasures in advance, in order to prevent botnets from taking advantage of individual endangered resources.

6.1 Future Trends

The future development of botnet technologies is hard to predict and various existing predictions have proven to be false already. While experts have predicted a large amount of botnets using resilient peer-to-peer architectures, the majority of current botnets still uses centralized C&C architectures. Even though peer-to-peer technology does provide significant benefits to botmasters, it is only used occasionally. A reason for this observation may be the higher complexity of peer-to-peer networks in contrast to rather simple and well-tried centralized approaches. Furthermore, technologies like domain or fast fluxing reduce the need for decentralized C&C network architectures. Finally, as long as simple and well-proven approaches still serve their purposes, there is no need to switch to more complicated or expensive approaches.

However, botnets are likely to improve even further on a technical level. This progress will especially affect the effort needed to analyze and counter future botnets. Whereas current botnets for example already rely on signed commands and strong encrypted communication channels, the underlying procedures are still not used correctly in many cases. The Waledac botnet for example uses state-of-the-art encryption techniques but lacks a proper implementation. As a result, the key used to encrypt the communication messages is always the same [66]. Once reconstructed, researchers were able to use this key to decrypt the entire communication. Programming flaws like that may be the result of malware authors lacking experience in using encryption techniques. For future botnets, it can be anticipated that serious flaws like that will happen less likely. Thus, botnets can be expected to use encryption techniques in a professional manner, which makes it harder for analysts to decrypt exchanged messages.

In addition to techniques complicating the analysis of a botnet's communication, future botnets will also rely on more sophisticated technologies used to complicate the analysis of their own binary code. Thus, obfuscation techniques used to

Table 6 Overview of different techniques to minimize the profit generated by botnets

Technique	Pros	Cons
BGP blackholing	Effectively mitigates DDoS attacks	Rather extensive collateral damage
Blacklisting	Selectively blocks known malicious resources	Only known sources are blocked
Port blocking	Can effectively mitigate various malicious activities within according networks	May mitigate legitimate activities as well
Walled garden	Effectively forces infected hosts to get disinfected	May have crucial side effects, may not be accepted by all ISP customers. Difficult legal situation
Encryption of information	Makes it difficult for botnets to access valuable information	Generates overhead in every day's workflows

massively increase the effort needed for reverse engineering are likely to occur in future botnets. VM packers that virtualize a bot's binary code by using an arbitrary instruction set in combination with a custom virtual machine are already used occasionally by malware authors. Since neither the virtual machine nor the virtualized instructions are known to analysts, this obfuscation technique massively increases the effort required for analysis. Commonly used packer distributions that are used to obfuscate a bot's binary code may eventually support virtualization, which might bring VM-based obfuscation techniques to the majority of future botnets.

Another trend that can be observed is that sandbox analysis will be used increasingly frequent in network security. Consequentially, malware can be expected to use even more sophisticated sandbox detection techniques, in order to prevent itself from being detected. If malware detects to be analyzed within a sandbox, it can for example idle in order to elude detection heuristics. Anti-sandboxing techniques like that are already used by various malware families and they are likely to be used even more frequently in future botnets.

With the increasing market share of operating systems like Mac OS X, it could also be observed that various botnets are starting to target these platforms as well. Furthermore, first cross-platform botnets have been discovered to target both, Windows and Mac OS X, platforms [67]. If this trend continues, it can also be assumed that an increasing amount of botnets will also target non-Windows platforms in near future. Despite different operating systems for desktop computers or notebooks, a significant rise of mobile could be observed. According to a recent report, the total amount of mobile malware has increased by more than 273 % comparing first half of 2010 and 2011 [68]. Targeting mobile malware offers various new opportunities to cyber criminals that can be exploited by botnets in order to generate revenue. Infected mobile devices can be used for example to intercept mTANs sent to mobile in order to legitimate fraudulent online banking transactions. Furthermore, mobile phones contain large amounts of valuable information like emails or contact data. Various mobile malware can also be observed to send SMS to premium numbers to directly generate revenue for the according provider. Mobile devices also offer cyber criminals the opportunity to track users GPS coordinates or spy on users using the mobile devices camera or microphone.

Whereas botnet construction kits were sold on the black market for some time, they are getting cheaper and easier to buy. This may lead to a further increasing amount of botnets used for example to generate revenue. Beyond that, botnets may be used increasingly in political context. Botnets may be used for example to launch DDoS attacks against servers of political opponents, for example to enforce individual political interests.

Due to recent progress in techniques to counter existing botnets as well as the willingness of responsible institutions to apply these techniques in practice, future botnets may become even more sophisticated. Furthermore, future botnets may use even more sophisticated attack vectors and C&C infrastructures. In this context, new botnets may further utilize social networks as part of their C&C communication. New botnets may also utilize cloud services or hosting as part of the C&C infrastructure.

6.2 Conclusion

The arms race between cyber criminals and countering organizations has spawned various sophisticated technologies. On the criminal's side, these technologies are used to increase the infection rate of new systems and to reduce the probability of being detected by antivirus solutions. On the opposite side, countering organizations have developed new techniques to detect current botnets one the one hand, and to actively counter existing botnets on the other. In this arms race, cyber criminals are generally one step ahead of countering organization. Mitigation technologies are therefore commonly developed as a reaction on novel offensive techniques utilized by detected botnets.

The enormous complexity of today's operating systems and software projects gives cyber criminals a strategically edge. Securing vulnerable systems requires eliminating all potential security flaws whereas cyber criminals only need to identify one in order to infect the system. By applying social engineering techniques, cyber criminals can even infect new systems without exploiting any software vulnerability at all. Security solutions therefore face a severe opponent, and have to make great efforts in order to protect individual systems from a multitude of different botnets. In this context, security solutions have to observe applicable law in order to combat active botnets whereas cyber criminals operate outside the law. Cyber criminals do not even have to face legal consequences, since they are commonly able to hide their identity with little effort.

Consequently, cost for setting up a new botnet are lower by orders of magnitude compared with the financial effort needed to apply individual countermeasures. Despite this effort, various effective countermeasures are available today that can be applied to actively mitigate the botnet threat. In this context, novel detection techniques in order to detect even previously unknown botnets as well as techniques used to actively detect infected systems of a particular botnet, have been discussed within this article. Furthermore, techniques used to analyze detected botnets, have been discussed subsequently. These techniques allow getting an insight into a botnets C&C infrastructure and spreading techniques as well as its operational background and purpose. By evaluating this information, active countermeasures can be developed. Various kinds of countermeasures to incapacitate or even completely remove active botnets were described. Additionally, techniques to prevent new infections as well as techniques to mitigate a botnet's malicious activities in order to reduce its profitability have been introduced. These techniques do not only imply technical countermeasures but also raising the awareness of individual users. Thus, it is possible to prevent a significant amount of social engineering attacks from being successful and even reduce the amount of information that can be extracted by botnets from infected systems.

Applying individual countermeasures however does not have a sustainable impact on the threat posed by botnets today. Taking down individual botnets does not prevent new botnets from emerging whereas preventing new infections will most likely result in more sophisticated attack vectors. In order to have a lasting impact on the threat posed by botnets, it is necessary to apply various kinds of countermeasures to mitigate botnets on all different levels. This cannot be done by technical approaches only but also requires end users being aware of potential threats. Consequentially, an integrated approach is needed, combining the effort of security companies, researchers, governments and initiatives. This includes raising awareness of end users, developing individual technical countermeasures and creating a legal framework, in which particular countermeasures can be applied. Within this legal framework, it has to be specified, which organization is responsible for the appliance of individual countermeasures. Therefore, a social dialogue is needed to provide for example law enforcement agencies with permissions that are generally accepted in order to effectively combat the botnet threat.

References

1. Leyden, J. (2009). The Register. [Online]. http://www.theregister.co.uk/2009/01/30/techwatch_ddos/.
2. Symantec. (2011). Symantec Internet Security Threat Report, Volume 16.
3. Edwards, C. (2011). Bloomberg. [Online]. http://www.bloomberg.com/news/print/2011-06-27/human-errors-fuel-hacking-as-test-shows-nothing-prevents-idiocy.html.
4. Lyden, J. (2005). The Register. [Online]. http://www.theregister.co.uk/2005/12/15/mcafee_internal_security_survey/.
5. Panda Security. (2010). The Cyber-Crime, Black Market: Uncovered.
6. Krebs, B. (2011). KrebsonSecurity. [Online]. http://krebsonsecurity.com/2011/06/criminal-classifieds-malware-writers-wanted/.
7. Krebs, B. (2012). Tagging and tracking espionage botnets. [Online]. http://krebsonsecurity.com/2012/07/tagging-and-tracking-espionage-botnets/.
8. Deibert, R., & Rohozinski, R. (2009). Tracking GhostNet: Investigating a Cyber Espionage Network. Information Warfare Monitor.
9. Sanger, D. E. (2012). Obama order sped up wave of cyberattacks against Iran. [Online]. http://www.nytimes.com/2012/06/01/world/middleeast/obama-ordered-wave-of-cyberattacks-against-iran.html?pagewanted=all.
10. Ottis, R. (2008). Analysis of the 2007 cyber attacks against estonia from the information warfare. *Proceedings of the 7th European Conference on Information* (pp. 163–168).
11. Leyden, J. (2010). The Register. [Online]. http://www.theregister.co.uk/2010/12/06/anonymous_launches_pro_wikileaks_campaign/.
12. Schmidt, J. (2007). The H Security. [Online]. http://www.h-online.com/security/features/Fast-Flux-747344.html.
13. Norton. (2011). Symantec.com. [Online]. http://www.symantec.com/about/news/release/article.jsp?prid=20110907_02.
14. F-Secure. F-Secure.com. [Online]. http://www.f-secure.com/v-descs/brain.shtml.
15. Munro, R., & Elmer-Dewitt, P. Time.com. [Online]. http://www.time.com/time/magazine/article/0,9171,968490-1,00.html.
16. BitDefender. (2010). Malware History.
17. Schauer, C. (2001). The Mechanisms and Effects of the Code Red Worm.
18. Ferguson, R. Businesscomputingworld. [Online]. http://www.businesscomputingworld.co.uk/the-history-of-the-botnet-part-i/.
19. Harley, D. (2009). ESET threat blog. [Online]. http://blog.eset.com/2009/07/07/guest-blog-how-much-spam-does-waledac-send.
20. M86 Security. Spam statistics. [Online]. http://www.m86security.com/labs/spam_statistics.asp.

21. Namestnikov, Y. (2009, July). The economics of botnets. [Online]. http://www.securelist.com/en/analysis/204792068/The_economics_of_Botnets.
22. Paulson, R. A., & Weber, J. E. (2006). Cyberextortion: An overview of distributed denial of service attacks against online gaming companies. *Issues in Information Systems*, 7, 52–56.
23. M86 Security. (2010). Cybercriminals Target Online Banking Customers.
24. Stevens, K., & Jackson, D. Dell SecureWorks. [Online]. http://www.secureworks.com/research/threats/zeus/.
25. (2009). Heise.de. [Online]. http://www.heise.de/security/meldung/Hunderte-Bundeswehr-Rechner-von-Conficker-befallen-195953.html.
26. Symantec Corp. (2010). W32.Stuxnet Dossier v1.3.
27. F-Secure. Worm:W32/Downadup.AL. [Online]. http://www.f-secure.com/v-descs/worm_w32_downadup_al.shtml.
28. F-Secure. Backdoor:W32/SdBot.MB. [Online]. http://www.f-secure.com/v-descs/sdbot_mb.shtml.
29. Kamluk, V. (2009). Securelist. [Online]. http://www.securelist.com/en/weblog?weblogid=208187897.
30. MessageLabs. (2007). Messagelabs Intelligence: August 2007.
31. Hypponen, M. (2008). News from the lab. [Online]. http://www.f-secure.com/weblog/archives/00001392.html.
32. Wisniewski, C. (2011). Naked security. [Online]. http://nakedsecurity.sophos.com/2011/09/07/an-analysis-of-the-pay-per-install-underground-economy/.
33. Holz T., Steiner M., Dahl F., Biersack E., & Freiling F. (2008). Measurements and Mitigation of Peer-to-Peer-based Botnets: A Case Study on Storm Worm.
34. Leder,F., & Werner, T. (2009). Know Your Enemy: Containing Conficker. The Honeynet Project.
35. Computer Security Group, UC Santa Barbara. (2009). Taking over the torpig botnet—my botnet is your botnet. [Online]. http://www.cs.ucsb.edu/~seclab/projects/torpig/.
36. Krebs, B. (2011). Krebs on security. [Online]. http://krebsonsecurity.com/2011/06/criminal-classifieds-malware-writers-wanted/.
37. Shah, C. (2010). McAfee blog central. [Online]. http://blogs.mcafee.com/mcafee-labs/zeus-crimeware-toolkit.
38. Leyden, J. (2011). The Register. [Online]. http://www.theregister.co.uk/2011/09/22/aldi_bot/.
39. Krebs, B. (2008). Washington Post. [Online]. http://www.washingtonpost.com/wp-dyn/content/story/2008/01/25/ST2008012501460.html.
40. Fisher, D. (2011). Threatpost. [Online]. http://threatpost.com/en_us/blogs/zeus-source-code-leaked-051011.
41. Mieres, J. (2011). Threatpost. [Online]. http://threatpost.com/en_us/blogs/ice-ix-first-crimeware-based-leaked-zeus-sources-082411.
42. Barford, P., & Yegneswaran, V. (2007). An inside look at botnets. *Malware Detection* (pp. 171–191).
43. Shadowserver Foundation. (2011, October). Shadowserver foundation—statistics. [Online]. http://www.shadowserver.org.
44. Damballa Inc. (2011). Top 10 Botnet Threat Report—2010.
45. Labovitz, C. (2010). Arbor networks security. [Online]. http://asert.arbornetworks.com/2010/12/the-internet-goes-to-war/.
46. Hogben, G., Plohmann, D., Gerhards-Padilla, E., & Leder, F. (2011). Botnets: Detection, Measurement, Disinfection & Defence.
47. Goodin, D. (2009). The Register. [Online]. http://www.theregister.co.uk/2009/04/16/new_ibotnet_analysis/.
48. Goodin, D. (2011). The Register. [Online]. http://www.theregister.co.uk/2011/01/19/mac_linux_bot_vulnerabilities/.
49. Maslennikov, D. (2011). Securelist. [Online]. http://www.securelist.com/en/analysis/204792168/Mobile_Malware_Evolution_An_Overview_Part_4.
50. F-Secure. (2010). News from the lab. [Online]. http://www.f-secure.com/weblog/archives/00002037.html.

51. Microsoft. (2011). Microsoft Security Intelligence Report Volume 11.
52. Porras, P., Saidi, H., & Yegneswaran, V. (2009). Conficker C Analysis. [Online]. http://mtc.sri.com/Conficker/addendumC/.
53. Stone-Gross, B. et al. (2009). Your botnet is my botnet: Analysis of a botnet takeover. *Proceedings of the 16th ACM conference on Computer and communications security* (pp. 635–647).
54. Kang, B. B. H. et al. (2009) Towards complete node enumeration in a peer-to-peer botnet. *Proceedings of the 4th International Symposium on Information, Computer, and Communications Security.*
55. Dittrich, D., & Dietrich, S. (2008). "Discovery Techniques for P2P Botnets.
56. Norton. (2011). Cybercrime Report 2011.
57. eEye Digital Security. Zero-day-tracker. [Online]. http://www.eeye.com/Resources/Security-Center/Research/Zero-Day-Tracker.
58. AV-Test.org. [Online]. http://www.av-test.org/en/statistics/malware/.
59. Fisher, D. (2010). Threatpost. [Online]. http://threatpost.com/en_us/blogs/possible-new-rootkit-has-drivers-signed-realtek-071510.
60. Botfrei.de. Anti-Botnet Beratungszentrum. [Online]. http://www.botfrei.de.
61. Tikk, E., Kaska, K., & Vihul, L. (2010). International cyber incidents—legal considerations. Cooperative Cyber Defence Centre of Excellence, Tallin, Estonia.
62. Leder, F., Werner, T., & Martini, P. (2009). Proactive botnet countermeasures—an offensive approach. Cooperative Cyber Defence Centre of Excellence Tallinn, Estonia.
63. Ramachandran, A., Feamster, N., & Dagon, D. (2006). Revealing botnet membership using DNSBL counter-intelligence. *Proceedings of the 2nd Conference on Steps to Reducing Unwanted Traffic on the Internet* (Vol. 2).
64. Schmidt, J. E. (2006). Dynamic port 25 blocking to control spam zombies. *Third Conference on Email and Anti-Spam.*
65. McAfee. (2011). Underground Economy—Intellectual Capital and Sensitive Corporate Data Now the Latest Cybercrime Currency.
66. Calvet, J., Davis, C. R., & Bureau, P.-M. (2009). Malware authors don't learn, and that's good! *Malicious and Unwanted Software (MALWARE)* (pp. 88–97).
67. Castillo, C. (2011, May). I smell a RAT: Java botnet found in the wild. [Online]. http://blogs.mcafee.com/mcafee-labs/i-smell-a-rat-java-botnet-found-in-the-wild.
68. Benzmüller, R., & Berkenkopf, S. (2011). G Data Malware Report January–June 2011, G Data.